222 TERRIFIC TIPS FOR 2

222 TERRIFIC TIPS FOR TWO

Caryl Krueger

ABINGDON PRESS
Nashville

222 TERRIFIC TIPS FOR 2

Copyright © 1995 by Caryl Waller Krueger

This book is printed on recycled, acid free paper.

Library of Congress Cataloging-in-Publication Data

Krueger, Caryl Waller, 1929-
    222 terrific tips for 2 / Caryl Waller Krueger.
        p.   cm.
    Includes index.
    ISBN 0-687-00776-3 (acid free paper)
    1. Marriage. 2. Communication in marriage. 3. Interpersonal relations. 4. Interpersonal communication. I. Title. II. Title: Two hundred twenty two terrific tips for two.
    HQ734.K963   1995
    646.7'8—dc20   94-39882
                                                                              CIP

The author has made every effort to make the information and suggestions in this book practical and workable, but neither she nor the publisher assumes any responsibility for successes, failures, or other results of putting these ideas into practice.

Other books by Caryl Waller Krueger include:

1001 *Things to Do with Your Kids* (Abingdon Press)
Working Parent-Happy Child (Abingdon Press)
The Ten Commandments for Grandparents (Abingdon Press)
101 *Ideas for the Best-Ever Christmas* (Dimensions for Living)
Single with Children (Abingdon Press)
365 *Ways to Love Your Child* (Abingdon Press)

95 96 97 98 99 00 01 02 03 04 —10 9 8 7 6 5 4 3 2 1

MANUFACTURED IN THE UNITED STATES OF AMERICA

This book is dedicated to

my Northwestern University freshman dorm mates:

Edith Anne, Betty Lou, and Ellen Sue

and the ideal men we met,

married,

and stayed married to these many years:

Chuck, Norman, Charles, and Cliff

Contents

You said "I do"....

On the memorable day when you said "I do," you probably had little knowledge of what that pledge would really involve in the years ahead. Having said "I do" *then*, you're faced with actually having to do it *now*.

This past year I studied strong and lasting marriages, researched marital problems, and interviewed successful marriage partners. In many ways I was surprised at how they described the strengths of their marriages—the bonds that held them together. It wasn't all roses!

In my survey I found marriages that endured job changes, money problems, bad habits, infertility, infidelity, children's deaths, obnoxious relatives, recessions, stress, rebellious children, boredom, illness, divorces followed by long-term second marriages, even a dog who tried to ruin the marriage! But somehow the marriages survived! (And so did the dog.)

History shows that when people stop marrying, their entire culture is in jeopardy—home and civic life crumbles, relationships flounder, and children suffer. So, good marriages are the glue that holds society together and makes for the continued progress of all humankind. In this way partners in a committed marriage have a positive effect on the future—thus the importance of learning why and how marriages succeed.

In today's society, marriage is frequently treated like Kleenex: use one, throw it away, try another. Yet statistics show that history often repeats itself in a second unsuccessful marriage, and thus it might have been an astute idea to work harder to keep the first partnership together. There are, of course, exceptions such as when abuse or violence within the family make ending the marriage the wise way out. But in most marriages, divorce results from an accumulation of small incompatibilities—problems that had they been addressed in a timely manner, could have been resolved, resulting in a satisfying relationship.

So what did the successful marriage partners in my survey *do* to turn their challenges into triumphs? You'll find out in their stories and their 222 practical suggestions. I'll share the most important ingredients in a lasting relationship, ways to keep the marriage together when you're wildly busy, and how to avoid the "Master Destroyers" of marriages.

The average marriage in my survey has lasted forty-three years, and with 486 people contributing, you're getting the benefits of 20,898 years of successful marriage experience within the covers of this book! So pay attention and learn from the experts who have proved that the vow "for better or for worse" can become "for better and better!"

Caryl Waller Krueger

When 486 people shared stories of their good marriages with me, I was touched by their affection for one another and their honesty about both problems and solutions. And so, I have fondly named these folks the "Fabulous 400." You'll meet them many times in this book.

As varied as the backgrounds of these couples were—they came from a rainbow of ethnic roots, socioeconomic groups, and living environments—the bottom line was their determination to "make it work." They didn't give up easily!

They share ideas from marriages as short as ten years duration to as long as sixty-eight years of togetherness and the majority have had more than twenty-five years of experience. So the Fabulous 400 know what they're talking about and are happy to share terrific tips with you.

In evaluating the concepts that kept them together, they

listed these positive elements as contributing most to their success:

- Frequent and honest communication
- A loving and caring relationship
- Unconditional trust
- The willingness to grow and change
- Satisfying ways of resolving arguments
- Good relationships within the family circle
- Enjoyable leisure time and good friends
- Effective use of time and sharing of work at home
- Sound money-management and financial planning
- A strong desire to make the marriage work

Now it's up to *you* to join the Fabulous 400 in building a long-lasting and happy marriage.

"Just talk to me!"

Donna decided that Bart really didn't care. Once again, after she'd rushed home from work, fed the kids, and prepared a special dinner for two, he'd turned up an hour late for dinner. He said he was sorry—sorry like the day he forgot to pick up Sarah at the library or sorry like the time he didn't make it to the town hall meeting she was chairing because he didn't think it meant that much to her. And this week, for several nights in a row she'd fallen into bed early—dead tired, and he hadn't bothered to ask why.

But worst of all, Donna was sure he didn't know how she felt: tired, rushed, hurt, angry—and so in need of his loving attention. How could he know since they had no time to talk? And she wondered if he too had desires and problems (ones she'd gladly listen to if there were opportunities to talk). But somehow communication had broken down, and their *marriage was breaking up because of it. She felt like screaming in his face: "Just talk to me!"*

Research shows time and time again that lack of communication is a prime cause of many divorces. Problems undiscussed and unsolved are one of the Master Destroyers in marriage, while the exchange of information strengthens the bond between husband and wife. Without communication the marriage reaches a point where one partner's life is almost a mystery to the other. And it takes on the aspect of secrecy where it isn't intended. Secrecy has no place in marriage!

"If only I'd known . . . " is a lame excuse. "If only I'd known what he was thinking (or planning or hoping or doing), we could have talked it over." The problem is how to know—how to find the time to know—what's going on in the thoughts of the one you love.

The Fabulous 400—a term for the 486 people who took part in my survey—listed *good communication as the number one ingredient in a strong marriage*. They said:

"We feel comfortable talking about any subject."

"The kids are often included in our conversations when the subject concerns the entire family. That way they also learn the importance of frequent and positive communication."

"We make sure we have an in-depth conversation every day. Sometimes we have to fight for the time, but we do it."

"No holding back for a better time—the better time often doesn't come."

Good communication in a marriage accomplishes many things. In the case of Donna and Bart, it could have solved many of their problems if they'd only talked about their busy lives and how they might help each other. It could have solved the problem of the uneaten dinner if Bart had thought to communicate his schedule. It could have solved the problem of Sarah's being abandoned at the library if they'd gone over their daily plans. It could have solved the problem of Donna's hurt feelings if she'd told him how important the town meeting was to her. And it could have solved the problem of her not knowing whether Bart also had worries that she could have listened to, sympathized with, and perhaps helped to solve.

But how to find the necessary time? Couples need both miniconversations (quick exchanges of information) and maxiconversations (calm, thoughtful talks). The miniconversations are great for reminders, coordinating events, and good wishes for the day. But the more important ones are the maxiconversations where the participants' true sentiments come to the surface to be shared. It is in these maxiconversations that we really communicate our present feelings. And, sometimes we develop new feelings, too, making us into more sensitive and interesting beings.

Whether you are a family of two or ten, it is imperative that your communication consists of both short one-liners and longer in-depth discussions. Your marriage will be better if you use both because communication is the oil that makes the engine of a marriage run smoothly.

MINICOMMUNICATION

It's unfortunate that there are so many occasions for injured feelings caused by the failure to share just a few words with a spouse. It is lovingly considerate to let each other know such simple things as where you are, where you are going, and when you'll return.

And, those "I'm sorry" lines won't be needed if minicommunication is used to remind each other of items to get at the store, little people to be collected, or the time a meeting starts.

While these brief chats will not result in profound thoughts, they will make marriage much more pleasant, and that is a big plus in this busy world. It makes no difference if you are newlyweds or senior citizens, you need to exchange information regularly.

The Fabulous 400 shared these ideas for minicommunication:

GIVE ME THIRTY SECONDS AT NOON   No **1** rational boss will deny an employee a once-a-day call to a spouse. A half minute doesn't sound like much, but you'll be surprised at all you can say in this brief time. One couple say they always look forward to this moment of togetherness in the middle of a busy day. They use it as a time to reaffirm their love, not in a routine way, but with a variety of little lines such as "Love you, see you soon" or a light-hearted "Try to be good until tonight."

FIFTY-FIVE MILES PER HOUR   Whether **2** you're creeping in traffic or flying down the freeway, car-talk is good for miniconversations. You don't want to distract the driver with talk about major political or emotional issues, but you can accomplish a lot in otherwise wasted time. If you're on the way to a social event, you can share good ideas on things to talk about there. And you can spend your car conversation time on subjects of importance to each other.

EAT AND TALK   Turn off the TV during **3** breakfast and dinner and talk to each other— and to the kids if they're on the scene. Listen to the radio or read the paper before the meal so you have some fascinating tidbits on which to comment. Teach kids to bring a conversational topic or question to the dinner table—and if they say they can't think of one, hand them the newspaper.

4 SHUT UP AND LISTEN   One couple suggested that each partner try to do only 49 percent of the talking. No fair hogging the conversation. Run-on talkers have the tendency to not listen while the other person is speaking, always waiting for a moment to leap into the conversation. Break this obnoxious habit! Listen until your partner finishes, then connect your comments to the thoughts you've heard.

5 SHARING   A husband said he avoided talk with his wife because he was "a man of few words." However, they were growing apart. He decided he'd strive to initiate pleasant conversation with her several times a day until it became more natural to him. In everything he did and in everything he saw, he tried to find things to share. Sometimes he read to her something that had interested him. Soon he found that small talk occasionally graduated into deep discussions where he shared his innermost feelings and concerns. Best of all, he was enjoying it!

6 SILENT COMMUNICATION   There are times when you can't talk, but you still want to communicate. Whether it's a reminder or a love note, communicate with a short message on the mirror, the pillow, in a pocket, on the car dashboard, or in a lunch box.

7 SPEAK LIKE SWEETHEARTS   Remember when you first fell in love? Remember how you couldn't wait to talk with your beloved and share sweet things? Well, if you're going to last until your golden wedding anniversary, you'd better continue to cultivate sweet feelings and the sweet words to go with them. Be sure that along with all the words about problems, there are words of appreciation, interest, concern, and love.

MAXICOMMUNICATION

To fully understand and appreciate each other, there have to be times during the week for in-depth conversations. In my survey, I asked couples how often they had a serious conversation with one another. The most common answer was once a week—and most couples regretted that they didn't talk more often.

One woman said that she got "all talked out" from dealing with the children all day long. She felt she might need a conversation course in order to communicate in an interesting way with adults. However, it is possible to become better at communication without going back to school.

Start by asking yourself these questions:

- Am I being so critical that conversation with me isn't enjoyable?
- Do I have a sense of humor and laugh at even the slightly funny things my spouse says?
- Do I read enough to be an intelligent conversationalist?
- Am I as pleasant in talking to my spouse as I am to my customers or friends?
- Do I give the impression that the conversation is tedious and I can't wait to get on to something else—like watching TV?
- Do I give answers that are an easy way out, rather than revealing my true feelings?
- Am I afraid of being frank or expressing a need?
- Can I keep a confidence, or do I repeat to others everything my spouse or friends say?
- Do I resent suggestions even when they're well intended?
- Does my conversation often deal in vague conjectures rather than solid facts?

- Do I have a tendency to talk only about gloom and doom, or do I also share some good news and good ideas?
- Do I ask intelligent questions about the other person's topic of conversation?
- Am I a multifaceted person, or can I only talk about weather and health problems?
- Am I learning new things every day that I can share?

• • •

Interaction with others is one way to gather ideas for conversation. When you only discuss work and family, the talk can become problem-oriented. Certainly there is a place for deep discussion regarding the progress of careers and of children. Those conversations are absolutely required.

However, for a strong marriage, you need to have conversations about the world beyond home and office. The substance of these talks comes from your activities in the community, your leisure interests, plus intellectual ideas you gather from classes, books, newspapers, and quality television shows. These topics require *your* thought—you can't just suck in the ideas of others. You need to process ideas, ponder them, refine them, and discuss them.

Think about your last social outing. Did the conversation around the table go beyond weather, sports, illness, and kids? If it didn't, it's time you introduce some new topics, or trade in your friends. Certainly light social talk is amusing and necessary, but you don't need to waste an entire evening with it.

Good communication abroad makes you a better person at home—a growing person. It keeps you and your spouse linked by language as well as by love.

For maxiconversations, here are some ideas:

8 **THE 3" X 5" CARD**   Keep a small card and pencil in your pocket or purse and also on your desk or counter. During the day, jot down any interesting subject that pops into your head. These ideas will give you topics for conversation that evening or in the days to come.

9 **JACUZZI OR BATH TIME**   There's something soothing about whooshing warm water that just brings out honest conversation. Give up the shower at least once a week in favor of a good soak-and-talk. Return to your own childhood when bath time was fun time, or to your kids' early years when you watched their water antics or read them a book. If you prefer to bathe alone, take a book into your tub and read, later sharing what you read with your spouse.

10 **WHAT COULDN'T WE SAY?**   A Fabulous 400 couple married over sixty years emphasize the importance of frankness in a marriage. She says they have cultivated the ability to talk to each other on almost any subject. In their six decades together, she says that there are only two topics that remain "off limits." On these they've agreed to disagree, and they find plenty of other things to discuss. Sometime ask your mate if there is any topic that you could not discuss together. Then see if you can find a way to occasionally talk about that topic in a nonjudgmental way.

11 **"NO AGENDA" TALK**   Sometimes it is refreshing to have a long conversation on a totally new subject—not one you've been mulling over. One couple says that these "no agenda" talks come from just sitting quietly holding hands until a subject comes to the surface. And they report that just silently being together is a form of communication, too. There's merit in a quiet moment each day.

12 **BACK RUBS**   When you're relaxed, the dialogue flows easily. One couple give each other a weekly back rub by candlelight. They find that talk comes easily in this calm atmosphere, even though the time required isn't more than about twenty minutes.

13 **CONVERSATION STOPPERS**   Marriages are in trouble when certain lines are used to hurt or quash discussion. Avoid lines that start like these: "I've told you before. . . ." "I don't want to hear about. . . ." "I don't care. . . ." "You always do that dumb thing . . . ." "When will you learn. . . ." "I'll never change my mind. . . ."

14 **ON THE ROAD AGAIN**   Travel is great for talk. When you're going on a long motor trip, plan ahead to discuss issues of importance to your marriage and family. Actually make a list of them and suggest that family members take the lead in introducing their own topics. Once when our family had a trip to a remote island with long days at the beach followed by uninterrupted dinners together and then quiet evenings without TV, we each prepared to talk on one subject. From my husband we learned about Kondratiev curves, and the kids educated us on such subjects as replacing car transmissions, doing magic tricks, the highlights of a philosophy course, and the writing of political "white papers." And my topic? Semantics and the art of conversation! There was no shortage of questions and give-and-take conversation.

15 **PILLOW TALK**   In the quiet darkness of the bedroom, good in-depth conversation can take place. Because you are probably tired, conversation in bed should not be combative, but rather supportive. "How are you doing at the office?" "What can I do to help?" "I appreciate your good ideas." And of course, "I love you so much." Don't just immediately turn over and go to sleep. Make this a time of loving communication.

 **16** **HELPFUL DEBATES**   A wife found that she seldom got to talk because her husband just arbitrarily made all the decisions without communicating with her. So, she suggested a weekly debate—the kind where each side gets to speak, then rebut, then summarize. That way there could be no filibusters. He reluctantly agreed and even let her select the subjects. He soon found that he enjoyed these opportunities "to think about and settle things."

17 **BE PREPARED**   *High quality* communication doesn't just happen—someone has to first think of a subject before the conversation can start. Suggest to family members that in order to have good communication they should have an interesting topic or two prepared for occasions such as mealtimes, long car drives, social events, and before-bed chats. Learning to communicate as a youngster will reap benefits in those business and marriage years ahead.

18 **UP WITH THE ROOSTER**   One couple has always set their wake-up alarm time for ten minutes earlier than necessary. They just lie in bed and talk. They say it is a wonderful, relaxing way to start the day.

19 **THE FAMILY MEETING**   Clearing the air once a week is a good idea for families of all sizes. When children are small, start a weekly get-together just to talk about common family concerns. Hold the meeting where there can be good eye-contact and comfortable seating. This isn't a session for tattletales or bawling out, but a civilized solution-oriented and educational dialogue where each family member can speak, question, listen, and understand.

20 "I" STATEMENTS   Communication can break down when one person attacks another with "You" statements, such as "You never do anything right" or "You always leave all the work for me." You'll get much further in healthy communication (and accomplishing your aims) if you make "I" statements—the kind that tell how you feel or what you want. "I was disappointed and sad about. . . . " "I need some help to get everything done." "I know this concerns you, and it concerns me, too."

21 WINDING DOWN   A working couple with three school-age children have found that they need a moment to wind down at the end of the day when they all return home. However, everyone is usually hungry for dinner and is bursting with talk. So, the first one home gets a light snack ready (a cup of soup, or crackers and cheese). Then while sitting and snacking on the porch, each family member has an opportunity to share the most important thing that happened that day. Having taken the time to wind down, they're now ready to read the mail, start dinner, do homework or chores.

22 NO TV DINNERS   When the TV is on, conversation is off. Make it a rule: dinner is eaten at a table without the intrusion of television. If you've become accustomed to silently eating in front of the TV, this may be a difficult transition at first, but once you realize the joy of talking together, you'll find that there is no shortage of good conversation.

●   ●   ●

The biggest problem to overcome in communication is the inertia of rest. Saying nothing, not talking, seems so safe. But by talking sooner, rather than later, you'll find that problems don't fester and become impossible to fix. Don't let things build up to a point where you feel like exploding. A frank dialogue may not always be pleasant, but it's far better than sullen silence.

Keeping in touch also means keeping in love. When you deeply care for another, you want that person to have positive self-esteem and to feel good about the marriage. You bring about this exhilarating feeling of well-being by communicating with each other.

And what about Donna and Bart whose story opened this chapter? They discovered their problem of noncommunication and didn't let it destroy their marriage. Years have passed and the marriage continues to be happy. And Sarah is no longer left waiting at the library—in fact, she's now in college.

To love and to honor . . .

Sam believed that he took his wedding vows seriously. He loved Meredith and felt she loved him, too. But after twenty-five years of marriage, two grown children, three job changes, and four household moves, the romantic spark was gone. He often forgot to give those good-bye and hello kisses, he realized he said "I love you" like a robot, and he admitted to himself that their sexual encounters were routine—performed as if they were scheduled therapy.

While he had always thought that when they had more time to themselves their love would grow, he found it hadn't, and now he wished he'd taken the time to give dimension to their love all through those twenty-five years.

Meredith was the more caring and passionate of the two. One day she commented on the lack of intimacy in their marriage, and although Sam *promised to be more attentive, she came to regret her action since she now felt he was just being rigidly dutiful. Romance was no fun if you had to legislate it! So, she gave up hope for a more loving relationship.*

Meredith and Sam each silently wondered if this was the way it was supposed to be, getting along, getting older, but no longer feeling that passion, that spark, that all-absorbing love.

Most couples will admit that keeping love alive over a long period of time takes thought and effort, and we're going to consider both of those later in this chapter. But first, I would like you to compile a simple list of reasons why you love your spouse. This is a bit like Elizabeth Barrett Browning's sonnet that begins "How do I love thee? Let me count the ways." I'm asking you to "count the ways" you love your partner.

To get you started, I'm providing a basic list. Cross out the ones that are not important to you, and add your own ideas. Then, total up the number of lovable qualities your spouse has. Unless this book is borrowed from the library, you can use this as your worksheet.

I love my husband/wife because he/she is:

1. Physically attractive, clean, well-groomed
2. Thoughtful, remembering special occasions
3. Sensitive, understanding my moods and needs
4. Romantic, in surprising little ways
5. Faithful, not playing around
6. Funny, at appropriate times
7. Physically fit, athletic
8. Intelligent, continuing to grow mentally
9. Good in bed, tender, satisfying
10. Optimistic and hopeful about the future
11. Affectionate, loving and caring of me
12. A good parent to our children

13. Concerned about our community and the world
14. Considerate of my family and friends
15. Not foolish about safety and health matters
16. Creative and open to my suggestions
17. Able to ignite a sexual spark in me
18. Articulate about his/her own personal needs
19. Successful in business (in a career away from home or the business of running the home)
20. Enjoyable to work with around the house
21. Honest in our relationship
22. A good friend
23. Kind, nonabusive
24. Spiritually minded, religious
25. Interesting to be with on a one-to-one basis
26. Free from obnoxious habits
27. Interested in similar activities
28.
29.
30.

Please make your list as long as possible! It would be helpful to have your spouse make a list too, and then compare them. This will help each of you learn what is important to the other and what is needed to improve the varied expressions of love in your marriage.

It is qualities like those listed above that make a person lovable. Love isn't gender-related—both partners should be lovable. The Fabulous 400 listed the traits they valued most in their spouse, and over half chose to describe their mate as their very best friend. A satisfying sexual partner was in second place for men, while women listed simple affection as second.

One man said "Friend and lover—that's an unbeatable combination!" *Statistics show that marriages last longer when mates are both friends and lovers.* Many of the qualities listed above could be applied to friends only, but an enduring marriage relationship goes beyond friendship.

It is important that you know *why* you love your spouse. A vague answer won't do. Finding the specifics and giving them regular thought will increase appreciation and love.

Love takes both thought and effort. With this list, you have started to think about why you love your partner. Thinking is essential to acting. When you realize all the different ways you love your spouse—as friend, lover, provider, partner, and so forth—your *appreciation* for your spouse will grow.

Of course, there are very few who embody all these sterling qualities, and if your list is shorter than a dozen, your marriage is built on too few bonds and thus it is more apt to fail. But don't despair. You can work together to lengthen the list of lovable qualities.

CAN A PERSON REALLY LEARN TO BE MORE LOVABLE?

Of course! We sometimes believe the line "people never change." However, clinical tests show that an improvement in character is possible no matter what the age. In my survey, respondents were asked if their partners had changed since marriage—changed for the better, for the worse, or remained the same. Over 90 percent said their spouses had become better through the years.

While research shows that women are the more caring and loving of the two sexes, there is no genetic reason for this. In the past, men who behaved in a tender and solicitous manner were sometimes considered wimpish, but that's no longer true today as men blossom as devoted friends, compassionate caregivers, and loving fathers.

Becoming more lovable and being able to give love are not magically endowed qualities. They are usually learned in childhood, but they can be enhanced in adulthood. Both children and adults learn love by example and by education.

If examples of loving behavior were not present in the formative years, the person may be unable to demonstrate love. However, loving role models, appreciation by the spouse for a more loving attitude, and psychological motivation can increase the ability to give and receive love.

Encouragement between husband and wife goes a long way in creating loving feelings and romance. Appreciation for expressions of affection will result in more affection. Suggestions for creative romancing will get a partner thinking of these on his or her own. Being aware of the needs of the other will increase loving conversation and activities.

We need to be mindful of the difference between love and sex. While love can be expressed at most any time and for an indefinite length of time, the sex act takes up an infinitesimal number of the minutes in each week. A strong and lasting marriage must be based on more than physical attraction, as necessary as that is.

There are countless ways to learn how to be more loving (books, classes, counseling, therapy), but loving must begin with the personal desire to do it. It must be thought of as one of the main ingredients in a strong marriage.

THE PHYSICAL SIDE OF LOVE

There are many physical ways to show affection. They include: kissing, hugging, holding hands, being physically close, having sex, going to romantic places, talking about love, and doing loving deeds. Concerning the relative importance of these, the Fabulous 400 men and women were quite different in their ratings.

Almost every male listed sex first, followed by kissing. However, women had surprisingly different preferences. They chose kissing, hugging, and physical closeness as the top three, and then sex.

Actually, an over-emphasis on sex can be damaging to a marriage, and can become a Master Destroyer. The excitement of new love and the attraction of sexual thrills can blind partners to the realities of everyday life and can even keep them from making intelligent decisions about their future. Sex can so take over a marriage that when it even slightly decreases in frequency and importance, the partners may perceive that the marriage is lackluster and boring. When sex is not supported by other loving acts, when speedy sex leaves one partner unfulfilled, when sex is selfish or used as appeasement or punishment, sex becomes detached from all-important love.

Marriage and family therapists have found that an excessively strong sexual urge may actually be something else: lust, a flight from loneliness, or a neurotic attachment. Statistics show that marriages based on physical attraction alone are more likely to fail in the first few years than marriages based on sex and affection.

THE IMPORTANCE OF AFFECTION

Whether you call it affection, caring, fondness, or tenderness, the act of expressing love (separate from sex) is the cement of a marriage. Each day is filled with opportunities for affection. But the affection has to be reality-based, not a sham. Rough, curt, nasty, and rude remarks kill affection. The manner of your ordinary speech to each other reflects your affection.

Your first words each morning, sleepy as you are, show your affection. "How's my love feeling this morning?" "You look great with your hair all tousled."

Your parting words express your affection. "Good-bye, I'll miss you." "I want you to have a great day."

Your greeting when you meet again at the end of the day verbalizes your affection. "It's been a long time without you." "I'm so glad to be home with you again."

The questions you ask illustrate your affection. "How did your day go?" "What can I do to give you a hand?"

The moments you spend concentrating on each other demonstrate your affection—small things like bringing a glass of water, or sharing a newspaper item that would interest your mate, or suggesting a step outside to look at the stars together.

The little things you do reveal your affection—making a favorite food, bringing home one rose, enfolding your mate in your arms when things are tough.

These seemingly minor signs of affection build one upon another to form a firm foundation for a loving, lasting marriage.

IDEAS FROM THE FABULOUS 400

Books, tapes, videos, and counseling can improve sex in marriage, but that is not the purpose of this book. However, the experiences of the Fabulous 400 can give you some ideas about how to express affection, ideas that can lead to more satisfying physical love.

Earlier in this chapter I said that love required both thought and effort. We've already talked about the thought; let's now consider how to make the effort. These ideas might take you from just thinking or talking about love to actually being that loving person by putting your words into action.

 **23** **USING THE L WORD** "I love you" can get a little routine if repeated too often, but "I love you because . . ." shows appreciation for something good that has happened and thus it encourages the good deed to be repeated. There is an infinite amount of love inside you, so don't be miserly about using the L word often.

24 **HOLDING HANDS** The touch of someone you love is so important; however, hugging and kissing may not always be appropriate. But hand-holding can go many places. Instead of taking a spouse's arm when walking together, hold hands. Hold hands at the movie theater, at restaurants, at ball games, and even at church.

25 NO BARGAINING TOOL

Don't make affection—or sex—a bargaining tool. Don't get even for previous hurts by denying affection (or insisting on sex). When affection leads to sex, remember that the "inviter" has the obligation to satisfy the "invitee." The best sex is between two people who respect each other and are eager and willing to make love at the same time. Never try to make a deal by asking for affection or sex in return for some other favor.

26 OLD-FASHIONED ROMANCE

Remember those old movies where the lovers let romance build up to sex (as opposed to today's movies where two people meet and immediately fall into bed)? One Fabulous 400 respondent says that he and his wife rent videos of classic romantic movies and then recreate the love scenes from the movie in their own way. She adds that this can make one long and stimulating evening.

27 DON'T JUST ASSUME

One respondent (married over fifteen years) asked his dad (married over fifty years) how he kept the spark of romance alive. "Never assume" was the dad's short answer. "Assume what?" asked the son. "Don't assume she knows where you are, where you're going, when you're returning, what you want to eat, and most of all, how much you love her. Even after 50 years, I still grab her and tell her why I love her with the same fervor I had when I was your age."

28 **PUBLIC PRAISE**   Don't keep your affection for your spouse to yourself. It's fine to express it and show it in front of the children, your grown-up children, and your friends. Once at a party, a wife was surprised to hear her husband saying, "Well, let me tell you the loving thing Alicia did for me yesterday . . . ." Although Alicia blushed a bit, she loved it!

29 **LOVING TRADITIONS**   In marriage, there are some "always" things that show you care. A young wife always puts a love note in with her husband's lunch. A retired husband always brings a wake-up glass of orange juice to his wife's bedtable each morning. A thirty-something couple always has a last dance in the bedroom before retiring for the night.

30 **PET NAMES**   A young married couple has decided to come up with a new pet name for each other for every year of marriage. They're keeping a list to share with their own children when they marry. This year they're celebrating their eleventh anniversary and call each other "Sweet-stuff." Previous pet names include Love-bunny, Sweetie-pie, Darling, The One Who Must Be Obeyed, Angel, Smoocher, Honey Bun, Beloved, Cutsie, and Precious Baby. They say it reminds them how their love changes (and gets better) with each passing year.

31 **LOVE OCCASIONS**   While birthdays, anniversaries, and Christmas are usual occasions for loving words and gifts, one husband makes sure that there is a love occasion each and every month. Obvious ones are Valentine's Day, Mother's Day, and Grandparent's Day. But he has invented holidays to go with the first day of each season: "*Spring*-into-Love Day,"

"*Summer*-Better-Than-Others Day," "I-*Fall*-in-Love-Again Day," and "*Winter*-Is-Cold-so-Hug-Me Day."

 **32** **TODAY'S NEED** A couple who both work in pressure-filled jobs take the time to eat breakfast and talk together before leaving for work. Each frankly admits what will make the day a success. Statements might be: "I need to really work fast." "I need one good idea." "I need to get along with Joe." Then, as they go their separate ways to work via carpool and bus, they think about the need the other has expressed. Invariably, by the time they reach work, they have come up with a helpful idea and telephone it to their mate. The wife says, "We love each other too much to ignore each other's needs and have them go unfilled."

33 **THIS ONE DAY** For just one day, determine to accept your mate. Don't complain, correct, preach, push, or judge. If you succeed for this one day, see if you can do it for two. Soon you might get the knack of focusing on important things, rather than picking on little things.

34 **ACROSS THE CROWDED ROOM** A simple signal can often be romantic. One couple uses the wink. When they're at an event —business or social—and one catches the eye of the other, they exchange winks. Most others don't catch this secret signal that means "I love you."

 **35** **WHAT'S THE CHOICE?** A magazine survey asked parents what they'd do if they had a few free hours. In order of popularity, these were the top choices: a movie, a restaurant, and sex. Almost half preferred going out to staying home and making love! And

20 percent said they'd rather just talk. A couple shouldn't have to choose, for the ideal marriage has a combination of social events, good communication, and lovemaking.

36 **A TINY INVESTMENT**   At a florist or novelty store, find an attractive small vase that will hold just one flower. This is a reminder of your love and should be placed on your spouse's desk, dresser, night table, bathroom counter, or other place where it will be seen. While it should be pretty enough when empty, the idea is to fill it often with a flower from your garden, a wild flower, or a purchased flower.

37 **NO EXCUSES**   Head to your card shop and stock up on birthday and anniversary cards, but also some friendship cards with sentimental messages and clever pictures, and even some blank ones where you can write down your own feelings. Next, go to the post office and buy some "love stamps" or other pretty postage stamps. Keep some cards at work and some at home, but most important don't wait for a special occasion to give or send them. Receiving an "I Love You" card on a dreary or busy day can be refreshing. And, when a birthday or anniversary does come around, you won't have to make up some phony excuse for not having a card ready.

38 **HIDING PLACES**   The most ordinary gift or simple card becomes a romantic message if you put it in an unusual place and wait for your loved one to find it. Consider these locations: in the car glove compartment, in the refrigerator, inside the newspaper, in a briefcase or purse, in the dog's bed, in the pocket of a robe, under the covers at the foot of the bed, on top of the ice cream carton, under the dinner plate, in the morning cereal box. Come on, don't just put it on the pillow—be original!

39 **THE ENVELOPE TRAIL**   When you have to be parted for a week, write short provocative messages and seal them in envelopes. Put on the outside the date for each day you'll be gone, then tie them with a bow, and leave them where they will be found. These one-a-day love notes will be reminders of your affection when you're away.

40 **PARTY PROMISES**   Write down a romantic promise on a small piece of paper and carry it to an event you'll both attend. Halfway through the event, slip it to your loved one. It doesn't matter if others see you do this (but they shouldn't read it). It will give them something to think about when they see the smile on your partner's face!

41 **WALLET INFO**   Keep a 3" x 5" card in your wallet that gives all the particulars of your beloved—shirt or blouse size, dress or pants size, glove size, hat size, shoe size. Now, you can go into any store and be 90 percent sure of buying something perfect. And you won't have to embarrass yourself by pointing to a salesperson and saying "About that size."

42 **OUR TOWN**   It doesn't make a difference if you live in a small town, the suburbs, or the inner city. Make a list of the twelve most romantic but inexpensive places you know. If you need help, read the newspaper entertainment and activities section, or ask friends. Then, write the twelve choices on slips of paper and put them in an envelope. On the first day of each month, together draw one out. That's the place to go for this month's romantic "date."

•   •   •

Sam and Meredith, the couple whose story opened this chapter, did eventually find the way back to romantic love, but it took time. It started when they went away for a marriage encounter weekend with a church group, but each admitted that their new and more loving relationship was comprised of many little things that they learned to do for each other.

Commitment to marriage is absolutely essential; it can't be a temporary feeling there one day and forgotten the next. It is easy to be committed when things are going well, but it is crucial to be committed when the marriage road is bumpy. Marriage is not the answer to finding happiness; marriage is the result of finding happiness.

There is no empirical evidence that there is a "one and only" right person in the world to marry. There are many individuals to whom a person can be happily married. And, while one does not marry with the idea of "improving" the partner, you should expect to both grow in the relationship. In the same way, a well-nurtured marriage grows in love with each passing year.

Trust is a must

It just sort of happened. At least that's what Anne told herself. Les's work hours were long, and that left crowded weekends when he would play with the kids, accomplish some basic home maintenance, and they would have rushed and sleepy sex. It seemed that they had little or no opportunities to talk at a time when she needed bolstering in her new job. At first, Martin filled those needs during their several-times-a-day talks at the office. Then it was lunch. Then it was a motel. And through the months that followed, Les seemed oblivious.

Then a "friend" who had seen Anne and Martin at a restaurant clued Les in as to what was going on. He couldn't believe that his angelic, church-going wife and the caring mother of his children was having an affair with an office colleague! Suddenly it dawned on him why she'd been coming home late from work, yet calm, happy, and contented. But

worst of all, when confronted with it, she didn't seem eager to end it!
More of this true story later.

When an affair becomes known, the feelings—on both sides—are mentally and physically intense. For example, after a husband has had an affair, he often has feelings of guilt, regret, or self-righteousness (since he reasons he had some justification). At the same time, the wife must deal with bitterness, doubt, and sometimes hatred. She wonders if he has done this before—and if he'll do it again. She feels duped—or even stupid for not having realized what was going on. But the biggest erosion is to the mutual trust— the backbone of the marriage that should exist between husband and wife. The usual result of an affair is that it is hard for either partner to ever trust the other again. Somehow, the marriage is bent out of shape and the close twosome just become two individuals living under the same roof.

Infidelity *(which can be tied to problems such as sexual incompatibility, marital boredom, excessive flirting, and irrational jealousy) is the second most common cause of divorce.* (Money problems are the number one Master Destroyer in marriage and we'll discuss those in chapter 9.)

So, how do affairs start? What are ways to avert them? Do they have to result in a broken marriage? Can the partners regain their balance and put the affair behind them?

NOT JUST HUSBANDS

The Fabulous 400 had a lot to say about trust versus infidelity. Although most people think that husbands are more inclined to have affairs than wives, my survey showed a near equal number of wives who had affairs.

A telling question on the survey was: "Do you wish you'd had an affair?" Far more women than men said "yes" to that one. And one respondent said, "I certainly would have if I'd had the opportunity."

Wishing to have an affair—but not doing it—can also be upsetting to a marriage. Longing for another person results in inattention to the person at hand. This is called *emotional infidelity* and needs to be treated as specifically as physical infidelity.

Over half the surveyed men believed their wives didn't know about their affairs. But, many wives admitted on their confidential questionnaire that they did know, but chose not to reveal it. On the other hand, the majority of husbands whose wives had affairs were totally unaware of that fact. These statistics might lead one to think that men assume that they are clever enough to get by with an affair, or that men are more gullible and self-absorbed than women and don't know what's really going on. I leave making such conclusions to you!

A major fact that every married couple has to face: love and sex are not the same. Yet, in the minds of many, they are. More men than women think "I have sex with my wife; that should tell her I love her." Meanwhile women long for intimate times with or without sex. They are often very satisfied with physical closeness—just holding and hugging.

Les and Anne's story is typical of what happens in a marriage after the early romanticism wears off and the business of making a living takes over. Les equated sex with love. He liked sex, but he and Anne didn't talk about it, they just did it. As the years passed and their personal lives became busier, even the less physical aspects of love and caring—the touching, holding, talking—ceased. While this didn't bother Les, Anne was frequently lonely and discontented. And so Anne was vulnerable to the thrill of having an affair.

WHAT'S THE BEST WAY TO AVERT AN AFFAIR?

The Fabulous 400 married couples in my survey had some good ideas. Here are the best:

43 **A Frank Discussion**   After marriage—but even better before—have a frank discussion about infidelity. It's certainly easier to talk about it when you're happily in love. What do your marriage vows say about commitment? What are some of the partnership essentials you expect your spouse to fulfill? Will you be forthright if there are unfulfilled needs? Does one spouse want to know if the other feels tempted? Can you speak candidly about your innermost feelings?

44 **Warning Signs**   Be alert to these signs of impending danger. For the spouse being tempted, be wary of someone who continually and privately seeks you out for counsel, who gives you secret looks and touches, or makes trumped-up opportunities to be totally alone with you. More danger signs: out-of-the-ordinary phone calls, invitations to "just" get together, business trips that will bring the two of you together, or the temptation to fantasize about making love to the other person.

For the spouse being duped, be wary of frequent late work hours or out-of-town trips, lame-sounding excuses for absences or unaccounted-for time, odd phone calls and hang-ups, and of course the old "lipstick on the collar" or a strange scent of perfume or aftershave.

45 **Direct Action**   When tempted, try to remove yourself from the enticement before it gets overwhelming. Make it a point to keep clear of the other person, to the point of altering your jogging route, your work routine, or your lunch habits. When you know you are going to meet, try to be in the company of another person so that there are three of you, rather than just two. If your spouse is not the type to get confrontational, mention the temptation to your spouse so that you get some moral support in fighting it off. Some people have even changed their jobs to get away from an impending affair. Make a special effort to reinforce your loving relationship at home.

46 **CURB JEALOUSY** From my survey, about 10 percent of married couples find it difficult when someone admires their spouse. This kind of attention is usually not an invitation to an affair, but sometimes a spouse responds to the situation with such irrational jealousy that it makes the other spouse take a second look. In these enlightened times, we should be able to have friends of the opposite sex without being suspected of infidelity, and in these cases you alone are in control of the boundary between friendship and infatuation. When men leer at women's figures or when women drool over men's muscles, it may cause jealousy for the marriage partner or it may indicate an unfulfilled desire.

47 **INTELLIGENCE BREAKS** Affairs can start when married life gets stagnant, but this doesn't need to happen if each partner is growing each day. (You can read more about this in chapter 4.) But one stay-at-home mother who felt she wasn't as interesting as the women her husband met during his business day decided to tackle her inadequacies. No matter how busy her day, she gave herself two fifteen-minute "Intelligence Breaks." The first was a time to read a chapter of a book on a topic that interested her—modern art, the Civil War, and hiking in the Himalayas were the first subjects she undertook. The second late-afternoon "Intelligence Break" came before dinner when she listened to the radio news as she changed out of her work clothes. Thus, when her husband arrived home tired but ready to talk about the day, she too was eager to share both the home news and the results of her "Intelligence Breaks."

48 **BE ON GUARD FOR THE "EX"**   That's what one husband in my survey insists! When there are children (or difficult financial matters to resolve), it may be necessary for a man (or woman) to be in contact with the former mate. This husband suggests his "threesome" method of handling this problem. When there is a phone call from the ex-wife, he tells her his second wife will pick up the extension phone to listen in and add any comments. When he needs to visit his ex-spouse at home, he always takes his wife along. He says, "It's not that I'm tempted by my ex-wife, but this gives peace of mind to my wonderful second wife, and it reminds my first wife that our relationship is now strictly business." And he adds that his second marriage has already passed the fifteen-year mark.

HOW DO AFFAIRS START?

Few spouses purposely set out to have an affair. Infidelity usually comes about slowly, one step at a time. Yes, there are a few occasions of instant infidelity such as when a person meets someone at an out-of-town convention and they end up in bed that night (a stupid move with the threat of AIDS). But that's not as common as the slow buildup to an affair.

Sometimes affairs begin with husbands and/or wives who were not ready for the commitment of marriage. They may have tested the idea of marriage by living together, and then after the test, they slid into marriage. But cohabitation is not a proving ground for marriage. Studies have shown that the divorce rate is higher for couples who live together before marriage.

The commitment to be married appears to be more difficult for men than women. This is especially true for those men who go into marriage with the idea that if it doesn't work, they can be satisfied with a secret, long-term affair or

divorce and remarriage. Women usually have a more roman-
ticized view of marriage and when problems arise, they are
more patient in trying to work them out together or in counseling. But eventually, they too can succumb.

And so, infidelity usually starts with some unfulfilled need
at home. One spouse is extremely busy and preoccupied with
other activities. Maybe there is little verbal support for each
other, resulting in the lonely spouse's feelings of low self-
worth. Perhaps fidelity to the marriage covenant was never
considered important. Or, marital relations may have become
a boring and predictable routine.

Next someone attractive comes on the scene. This person
fills these unfulfilled needs through attention and supportive
conversation. Then the magic of the first touch takes over—
often unintentionally as their hands accidentally meet at the
watercooler or the supermarket, or their shoulders touch in
an elevator or carpool. Looks are exchanged and signals sent.
The message is, "I'm interested."

Often at this point there is a waiting period. Usually an
adulterer *does* have a conscience, and at this point the merits
of going ahead with an affair are often carefully considered.
There may be a halfhearted attempt to make the home situation work better. And when that doesn't happen, self-justifi-
cation sets in and the affair takes a sexual turn. Once this
step is taken, repeat encounters occur, each with more
heightened anticipation and satisfaction. Soon there are
thoughts of divorce and remarriage so that this new wonderful relationship can go on forever.

Well, let's face facts. Statistics show that marriages that are
the outcome of an affair result in a higher rate of divorce than
first marriages. If you have an affair with someone who is
cheating on a spouse, that person has ample practice in
cheating and it may not be difficult to cheat on you next. But,
in the heat of passion, people don't dash to the library to
check on such statistics.

DO AFFAIRS HAVE TO RESULT IN BROKEN MARRIAGES?

While they often do, many sincere couples have worked out the problem and regained a strong and loyal marriage that has continued to be satisfying for many more decades. One woman tells this courageous story:

"For years, my husband had a long-standing affair with another woman. Somehow he was able to keep it completely secret from me. At last it became so grievous to him that he let it all spill out. While it was a terrible shock to me, I also felt great compassion for him since it had hurt him, too.

"I realized that I still felt a deep love for him. I felt I could and should give him the praise and support he needs. Unfortunately I find it easy to criticize and this was very painful to him when I did it on a regular basis. I thought he knew I loved him and was just trying to help him.

"We discussed the situation. I told him I would understand if he decided to leave me for the other woman. However, it was not my decision to make; it was up to him.

"At this point, his main concern was not my critical attitude (which I promised to leash) but rather whether I'd ever be able to forgive him and have a good marriage after this incident. With all my heart I assured him that I could forgive him if he chose to keep our family intact and give up the other woman. Although he admitted that he had great rapport with this person and she made him feel wonderful, he also expressed appreciation for my good traits.

"His decision was to break off the affair and work together with me to make our marriage a strong one. It wasn't easy at first, but with prayer and diligence, we achieved an even better marriage than before. I have put the problem behind me and tried to be a better partner, expressing more appreciation for his splendid qualities.

"While it took me longer to forgive the other woman than to forgive him, I finally was able to do that, too. Because he is such a great person, I can somewhat understand why any woman would love to have him.

"I do trust him and we don't even refer to the affair anymore. He has the amazing ability to let the past be past and not hold on to it. I'm learning to do this and find that *now* is what we have to work with. By the way, our marriage has now passed the forty-year point."

•   •   •

This ability to totally forgive a deep injustice is the main ingredient in helping a partnership regain its balance and put behind the affair. While the trust may be a bit tentative at first, with honesty it can grow and be even stronger than before the affair. The woman in this story learned that her continuous criticism could be curtailed or expressed in a more helpful way. But most of all, she learned to forgive and forget, one of the outstanding lessons in any life.

Unfortunately there are those cases where the spouse denies the affair, despite overwhelming evidence. This refusal leads to a huge loss of trust. And it brings out the "watch dog" syndrome in the injured spouse who looks for concrete reinforcement of his or her suspicions. Usually honesty is the best policy: bring it into the open, talk it out, make some decisions, and get on with a better life.

If there has been an affair in your marriage, these ideas may help to mend the hurt, and they may even bring you closer together than before.

49 **FINDING NEW THRILLS**   Participants in affairs say that one of the so-called thrills is doing something on the sly—outwitting others and getting by with it. My advice: find new ways to get your thrills—take up roller-blading or hot-air ballooning or find an all-consuming hobby to keep your mind (and body) busy. One man in my survey said he found great satisfaction in refinishing the bedroom dresser and headboard after his affair went sour, an affair that actually took place in their own bedroom while his wife was away at work. His wife agreed that both they—and the bedroom—needed a fresh start and so she bought a new bedspread and made matching valances to enhance his work. Thus, they started over in a like-new environment, which revitalized both of them.

50 **IT IS NOT YOU**   Avoid the tendency to take all the blame yourself if your spouse has had an affair. Certainly make changes in areas where you could improve as a person, but avoid accepting all the responsibility and the subsequent anger and guilt. Rather than mulling over what you might or might not have done to avert the affair, spend that time mending the marriage. Remember to be good to yourself!

51 **TWO-SIDED GRIEVING**   When an affair ends, there is grieving on both sides. For example, if a husband has had an affair, he may grieve for his separation from the other woman, or for the hurt he has caused his wife and family, or for the love he will no longer know, or for having made a mistake. The wife also grieves for the loss of innocence and trust in the marriage, or for her own hurt feelings. It is important that the grief be recognized, then handled, then forgotten.

52 **NOW WHAT?**   If the affair was the result of some dissatisfaction in the marriage, the essential step is to find a better way to deal with the elements you don't like. If you don't remedy marital challenges, there may be repeated affairs. Talk with your spouse about the things that genuinely displease you and together find ways of controling negative emotions and actions.

 **53 Don't Get Even** When a husband discovered a wife's affair, he was so angry he decided that the best tactic was to have an affair himself. Fortunately his wife decided to end her affair, they went for joint counseling, and he has never carried out his threat. Two wrongs never make a right!

54 Eliminate the Negative An old song gives some good advice: "Accentuate the positive, eliminate the negative, latch on to the affirmative, and don't mess with Mr. In-Between." You won't be able to eliminate the negative if you let it continually eat at you, devouring your time for positive thinking and affirmative action. It is good mental exercise to put it behind you. When the affair is over and you have satisfied each other as to your trustworthiness and forgiveness, stop bringing it up. Pledge to yourself that no matter how angry you get on any subject, you will never ever throw up this infidelity to your spouse.

55 No Double Standard There is nothing gender-related about infidelity. Men's hormones don't rage any more than women's. For centuries we've excused men's affairs on the basis that "men must be men." Yet when women have affairs, they're considered over-sexed sluts. Such reasoning is ridiculous because extramarital affairs are not natural or necessary for either sex. Don't hide behind this outmoded double standard.

56 Actions Speak Louder Than Words Couples in marriage therapy find that *acting* dedicated often makes them *be* more dedicated. After the affair, a wayward spouse may mouth fidelity. Acting the part of faithful spouse comes next. But the true test is not acting but *being* mentally and physically trustworthy.

57 **WORDS OF LOVE** A husband was astounded when returning some library books for his wife to find a love note tucked inside one of them. He didn't know the man who had written the passionate letter, but it made him realize how deficient he himself had been concerning words of affection. So, he started his own little campaign of love messages to his wife, leaving them in the kitchen cupboard, in her purse, on her night table. The library book love note was never mentioned. He knows his wife is totally committed to their marriage, and they just celebrated thirty-five years together. At the anniversary dinner, his wife gave a toast to her husband and told their friends how much she cherishes the love notes he writes to her. And the husband has realized that he long ago stopped worrying about who wrote the note or even if it was intended for his wife.

•   •   •

Much research has been done as to what triggers an affair. Many indicators point to the passages in life. Passages are events where we pass through a challenging experience and our lives turn a corner. These might be a household move, a new baby, a job promotion, the death of a parent. During these passages, one spouse is busy with a demanding project (packing the house, caring for the baby, getting accustomed to the new job, settling the estate) and the other spouse may feel lonely and emotionally adrift. But passages can and should be opportunities for being loving and supportive of the mate if these events are recognized as temporary occurrences.

Sometimes an affair is due to the inappropriate handling of stress. In midlife, affairs can flourish because of the pressure of succeeding at the office where the new college grads are moving in, thus leaving older workers with the feeling that they aren't as essential or powerful as they once were. Or, there is the stress of sending off the kids to lives of their own, a stress which brings on a deep feeling of emptiness that sometimes goes unnoticed by the other spouse. So, an affair fills the void.

However, in a marriage where there is good communication, these feelings of insecurity or loneliness or boredom can be voiced and the answers found with new activities to fill the void, and renewed love and companionship between spouses.

•　　•　　•

Now back to Anne and Les whose story opened this chapter. When the good "friend" revealed the affair to him, Les was stunned and found that all he could do was rant, rave, and stuff himself with doughnuts. For a while he felt he actually hated Anne, and didn't even want to look at her. He was in such a state of shock that he took a leave of absence from his job and went to visit his folks for a week. He knew that if he stayed in town, he might lose his cool and smash in the other guy's face.

When he returned from the trip, he had to face Anne who promptly disintegrated into tears. She, too, had spent time in quiet thought and an assessment of the problems and possible solutions. She realized that she had truly missed him. She understood that because of her easy solution to the problem of loneliness, she had inflicted a tremendous injury to both of them. He in turn admitted that he had been partially at fault for not being sensitive to her needs. At this point, Anne accepted the blame and asked his forgiveness.

And she also realized that she had to forgive herself if she was to go forward.

Later that same year there was a trial separation, but it only lasted a week before Anne and Les reunited. They agreed that such a love as they shared shouldn't be tossed aside, that they were wise enough to work out their problems. Fourteen years have now passed. The children have left the nest, and Anne and Les have found new joys in being a twosome again. The marriage was saved.

Growing up with your spouse

It's been over a decade since the storybook wedding of Hannah and Max. They returned home from their Hawaii honeymoon to a cozy love nest apartment and a life that was fun-fun-fun, just as it had been during their dating years.

Now, twelve years later, they have a small house with a big mortgage, a slightly dinged mini-van, the athletic boy and the darling girl they had always wanted, and secure jobs bringing in adequate income. With all this, you'd think they'd be exceptionally happy. But about a year ago they looked closely at their marriage and realized that they were not exceptionally happy or even slightly happy.

This unsettled feeling of discontent wasn't leading toward infidelity or divorce—they rarely had disagreements and they loved each other deeply. But they perceived that they were spinning their wheels and going *nowhere fast. One day was almost identical to the next and they wondered if the future was going to be any better. Fortunately they were good at communicating with each other, so for several evenings after the kids were tucked in, they talked about the future, what was meaningful to each of them, and just what their married life was all about.*

These talks lead them to some conclusions that they have been putting into practice for nearly a year. Even though little has changed regarding their jobs or possessions, they report that they now have a very happy and contented life. There was no magic wand, just the determination to enjoy life now—rather than waiting for some faroff time. This decision to stop stagnation and keep growing each day rubbed off on their two grade-schoolers, making their lives better, too.

Max summed it up by saying, "Life now has direction and purpose—actually many purposes." And Hannah added, "What we're trying to say is that we've found that growing up is a continual process."

How does one continue to grow up? This chapter is based on some of the helpful ideas Hannah and Max discovered.

WHAT'S IT ALL ABOUT?

That's a familiar question in conversation and song. What is it that makes someone's married life so special that the relationship remains strong and enduring despite negative outside influences? Are there "how to" hints that can help?

The marriage that grows will be the marriage that lasts. But how can one keep growing with all the obligations of work, home, children, and community? Certainly it takes good time-management skills in order to make opportunities for this growth as individuals and as marriage partners. These opportunities don't just happen—one must plan ahead and set aside the all-important time.

If one is so overwhelmed with daily survival, there's little time for self-improvement or husband/wife progress. And if one isn't getting better, just getting older, it's a downhill slide that can lead to boredom and frustration—a Master Destroyer of a marriage.

No one can grow up for you. It's a do-it-yourself project. But growing up—and up and up—is the best and most exciting thing for you and your marriage. All through their youth, kids have parents telling them to grow up. What is most often meant is for the child to become more responsible.

THE FOUNDATION FOR GROWTH: RESPONSIBILITY

Being responsible sounds so grim, but it doesn't have to be! It is only the *basis* for growing. Being responsible means getting a handle on the routine things in life so that you have time left over for the good stuff. So, growing up into adulthood and marriage is founded on the premise of becoming responsible for your own actions. No longer are there parents or teachers to tell you what to do. And most folks don't want a spouse or a boss to take on that role. Thus, you have to want to be responsible all on your own. (Of course there are some people who prefer to be protected from life, to have all decisions made for them but this isn't really "living," it's merely existing.)

So, what are you responsible for? What you do, how and when you do it, what you say, what you promise, what you think—in effect the whole of your life. But as a grown-up, you might not have those nagging reminders to heed—no one's watching over you. You can party all weekend if you want. It's your life. Waste it if you dare.

Some people get stuck in the age-twenty mode. They are cocky, think they know it all, and believe they don't owe anyone anything. The world is there to serve them. These individuals should not marry because they aren't ready for the responsibilities and exhilaration of coexistence with another adult. If you think you are "all grown up" in your twenties, just wait! There are many surprises ahead.

Fortunately, Americans are marrying later than ever before. The median age for first marriages in the U.S. is now 26.5 for men and 24.4 for women—an increase of three years since 1975 for both men and women. This increase ties in with a slight decrease in the divorce rate since the couples marrying are now more mature, more "grown up," more responsible, and more responsive to the world around them.

With marriage comes responsibilities—to your mate, your family, your job, and, most important, to yourself. It's much more than fulfilling the assignment of getting the garbage out on time. It is the art of using to the fullest what you have to work with: yourself.

GROWING UP, NOT GROANING UP

And what is growing? It is the continuous maturing or seasoning that should go on all through life. Seasoning is a perfect and descriptive word because growing is adding spice to your life. It is refining your character. It is self-improvement. It is honing of skills. It is reaching out to others. It is continually learning new things. It is learning to function both as an individual and as part of a marriage or family.

Growing up isn't a painful, groan-filled experience. It's a lot like the opening of a cocoon, long hidden in secret, now revealing the elegant, free-flying butterfly. This process of continually growing up adds wonder to a marriage year after year after year.

The Fabulous 400 in my survey felt that strong marriages are grounded on caring friendship and the bonds of love. Beyond these two important elements, they said that keeping mentally and physically active made for stimulating companionship. And in this area 91 percent felt that their mate had changed for the better during the years of marriage.

Developing together in the marriage is a day-by-day process. It isn't something you decide to do one day and easily achieve the next. It is composed of many little steps. Listen to the wisdom that these long-time marrieds share:

 58 FIND OPPORTUNITIES TO GROW How would you change your spouse if possible? Although the Fabulous 400 were rather well-

satisfied with their mates, they did have some ideas for improvement that fell into seven categories. (These were usually described as bad habits that weren't apparent early in marriage, but had subtly crept in as years passed.) These "opportunities to grow" are: physical inactivity, overeating and weight gain, disorganization, occasional inconsideration, pessimism, alcoholism, and stubbornness. These are certainly things that one can change if they are detrimental to a marriage.

59 LISTEN AND LEARN "I couldn't figure out how to find the time to read a book until my spouse started borrowing books record-

ed on cassette tapes from the library. I have a thirty-minute commute each way and listening to a good book makes the time fly. She carpools a different direction to her office and so we often listen to the same book, one being just a tape behind the other. This is just one of several ways we keep up with good literature and find we have common subjects to discuss."

60 JUST SAY "YES!" "When we talk about social activities we could do together, I sometimes feel that I'd just rather stay

home. But in our before-marriage counseling, the minister told us that we'd be happier if we remembered to give an enthusiastic 'Yes!' whenever possible, as long as it wasn't something unethical, immoral, or illegal. I've tried to follow that advice, and you know, some of the things I thought I'd hate (mountain hikes, Shakespearean plays, soccer) are now my favorites."

61 NOBODY'S PERFECT "The expectation of perfection is high when first married— that was true for us. Then, gradually, you

perceive a few faults. It shocked me at first to find that my husband wasn't flawless! And, of course, he pointed out several areas of my behavior that drove him up the wall. It seemed like a shattered dream until we talked about it. He then calmed down enough to explain that if we were both perfect, we had nowhere we could grow. So we made a list of the faults, decided which ones were unimportant and which ones we'd work on. Gradually many of our annoying bad habits disappeared. That was twenty years ago and we're still improving every day."

62 **SURPRISE NIGHT** "We feel that a date-night once a week gives us some activities separate from the kids. We usually plan together what we're going to do, but once a month it's a surprise. We take turns selecting an event, making the arrangements, and doing the driving. Our surprises for each other have included a moonlight picnic on a lake shore, a triple feature movie, a modern art exhibit, working with a group to rehab a house for a homeless family, attending a Scottish bagpipe concert, and visiting a worm farm. The last one was the weirdest surprise ever, but now, years later, it's part of our good date-night memories."

63 **SINGLE HABITS** "We were single, professional people for fifteen years before getting married. We were used to coming and going as we pleased, changing plans without a thought, paying no attention to time schedules, and keeping our apartment in its own private state of disarray. So, marriage was quite a jolt. In many ways we kept the independence we loved, but in some aspects we had to grow up out of our selfish ways. It's made us more considerate of each other, and consequently of our friends and our business associates. Yes, it was hard, but I now phone when I'm going to be late, apologize for stupid mistakes, and even gather the clothes off the couch before we sit down for the evening news."

 **64** **SCHOOL KIDS** "When I got out of junior college, I swore I'd never attend another class. School just wasn't for me. I got a good job and then married. Sharon is a wonderful person, a terrific wife, and she did a great job with our daughter. But Sharon has the biggest thirst for learning of anyone I know. After our daughter had married and left home, I gradually realized that Sharon did almost all the talking—while getting dressed, at the table, in the car, during TV commercials, when out with friends. My meager input was about my work and what was in the news, but that didn't make for very stimulating conversation. One autumn I went along with her to a school that offered adult education, sure it was going to be a bore. We each chose different classes but on the same night. It was great! We've been doing this for over ten years now, and becoming a school boy again has made the biggest change in my life. It's opened up so many horizons that I'm no longer hesitant or embarrassed to talk with people—or my wife."

65 **NOT BORING** "While I always thought I'd marry someone like myself, I ended up marrying someone quite different: in ethnic appearance, family traditions, religion, and profession. But we are alike in our extracurricular tastes such as cultural events, sports, and hobbies. Over the past three decades of marriage, we've found that it's OK to be different. We agree to investigate things we don't think we'll like, and we often find that our preconceived notions are wrong. Life together is certainly never boring."

66 **OTHER THAN TV** "My life had settled into a pleasantly dull routine—nine hours of work, then home for television with supper, helping kids with homework done in front of the television, reading the paper while watching television, and finally snoozing in front of the set. When taking out the trash after dinner, I'd often see a neighbor who'd ask, 'Whatcha doin' tonight?' I realized I always said the same thing, 'Watching TV.' This awakened me to consider what else one could do in the evening. At first I volunteered to read bedtime stories. Then the kids talked me into doing puzzles and playing games with them. Some nights I joined my wife who did step aerobics. Next thing I knew, I was refinishing a table top. And now, I'm building a model airplane that will actually fly—I hope. Not bad for a forty-five-year-old former couch potato!"

67 IN SICKNESS AND IN (BETTER) HEALTH

Marriage is actually good for your health. A study by the National Center for Health Statistics rated the health of about 120,000 married, single, widowed, and divorced Americans. Married men suffered less respiratory disease than single men, and married women had fewer accidental injuries. Married people have lower mortality rates for conditions such as stroke, influenza, tuberculosis, and almost all forms of cancer. While researchers don't know why marriage has a protective effect, they believe it may foster a healthier lifestyle, provide key psychological and social supports, and reduce stress. So, continue to encourage good health habits in your spouse as years pass.

68 WHAT I'VE ALWAYS WANTED TO DO!

Deep within each of us is some secret desire. Many of the married couples in my survey said that after the children were in high school and they had more time, they followed up on these desires that included getting a college degree, taking piano lessons, singing with a country-and-western band, setting up a model railroad, reading a ten-volume set of books by Will and Ariel Durant, going to baseball camp, learning to parachute, entering cooking contests, and taking up wood carving. Consider your long-postponed dreams, choose one, and indulge yourself.

LITTLE TREATS **69** "I knew that if our marriage was going to last, I had to learn to be more caring and appreciative of my wife. I'd come from a family that never gave compliments; we just griped when we didn't like something or we were silent when we should have been appreciative. I followed this inherited family trait without thinking of the confusion it caused my wife. When the pattern of silence became so annoying to my wife that she threw a plate at me, I realized that this was a place where I had to grow. As a grade school teacher, I often show my appreciation to my students by putting a gold star on a good paper. So that's where I began at home with my wife, actually putting a gold star on a piece of paper with a short note like, "Thanks for another good day together." Although she laughed at first, I could tell she liked it. Now we have many little treats we give each other as reminders that we care . . . things like one orange M&M on the pillow case, a flower at her place at the table, a new magazine from the newsstand, or a cupcake with a candle on it just before we watch the late news."

DO-IT-YOURSELF GROWING

In the first twenty-five years of your life, you acquired a lot of knowledge whether you realized it or not. You were forced to read many books, you took part in classroom discussions, you survived music lessons, you learned the rules of many sports, you mastered computer skills. But that was then and this is now. With a developing career, marriage, and family, the education process sometimes stops suddenly. Now your learning is focused on getting ahead at the office or combating a toddler's temper tantrums at home. While this is a form of growth, it's hardly the essence of true intellectual and cultural gain.

It used to be that husbands grew in knowledge by being out in the world while most wives stayed home and cared for house and children. This often resulted in women failing to grow and thus falling behind intellectually. Nowadays, many women are also growing in the workplace. And thanks to timesaving inventions, those working at home have opportunities to grow through selective radio listening, educational cassettes, and free-time reading. The care of children and home sometimes becomes a crutch for women who profess that they are too busy to do anything else. In most cases this is a lazy excuse. Many women manage job, children, and home and still find time to grow intellectually.

Sometimes when one spouse grows and the other remains stagnant in knowledge, the latter becomes a social embarrassment. But that doesn't have to be. Enjoying stimulating times together, being able to converse at social functions, having acceptable manners, dressing smartly (not necessarily expensively), introducing interesting ideas concerning the community, the nation, and the world—all these can be self-taught. After all, who wants to be considered dull!

What are some ways an adult can grow? From this checklist see how many suggestions are ones you're already doing to keep growing.

___ Reading a news magazine each week
___ Playing a wide variety of music on radio or stereo during dinner
___ Listening to the news while dressing in the morning
___ Regularly taking part in a sport such as tennis, hiking, or bowling
___ Visiting the library on a regular basis

__ Turning off the TV and reading a book
__ Joining a play or music series
__ Investigating different hobbies and trying some
__ Listening to Public Radio before bed
__ Following one commentator and taking part in a call-in show
__ Taking a class at a nearby college or university
__ Volunteering for a community service activity
__ Reading a current book on manners
__ Playing games and doing puzzles regularly
__ Joining a club that has helpful programs
__ Visiting a museum once a month
__ Joining Toastmasters and learning to speak effectively
__ Taking a ranger-guided park tour
__ Being active in church
__ Working for a candidate for public office
__ Volunteering at your child's school
__ Taking safety and CPR classes
__ Joining a garden club and improving your own garden
__ Teaching others a foreign language that you know
__ Writing your family's history

No doubt there are many more ways to enliven your life and keep growing, but these twenty-five suggestions should start you thinking. Don't leap into a bunch of them at the same time—try a few, then try others as you have the time. You can't help but grow!

DIFFERENCES

While marriage counselors usually recommend marriage between people who have many things in common, a strong marriage can result when the partners recognize and appreciate their differences (as in idea number sixty-five above). Over 65 percent of the Fabulous 400 felt that "thinking alike" was not as important as being willing to discuss differences and to try new things.

While differences are inevitable, it is important that the basic philosophy of the partners be similar; life aims and moral ethics need to be on the same wavelength.

The person you've come to know and love over the years of your marriage may be quite different from the one you married. This is more true of marriage partners under age thirty because they are not yet fully mature. Thus they change in many ways, some good, some possibly bad, and such radical changes in character can adversely affect the marriage.

However, with couples over age thirty, there are fewer character changes after marriage. "What you see is what you get," as the saying goes. Statistics show that these good mates just get better and better.

Differences can be accommodated when there is loving consideration of each other. One wife said that she feels sameness is better but when she and her husband have differences, she uses a technique she calls "Ignore and Endure." That may work for her, but learning to accept differences or to turn differences into a stimulating exchange of ideas is far better.

The next chapter gives specific ideas on how to settle disagreements. But remember, disagreements often arise when a couple fail to focus on similar things—where they are going together and how much they need to grow together in order to get there.

The etiquette of arguing

Kim looked at Tony as he came in the door. With a groan she said, "You forgot to pick up the dry-cleaning! You'd forget your nose if it weren't attached to your face." Tony shrugged his shoulders and responded, "So what, you don't remember anything you don't want to. You never even think to enter the checks you've written."

The simple quarrel escalated into accusations, demands, shouts, insults, anger—then hurt feelings, guilt, and stony silence—that was the sequence each time there was a disagreement between them. While Kim thought the cause was his fiery Italian temperament, Tony was sure it was her stubborn German background. But they soon realized it had nothing to do with their ancestors. It was just that each of them was headstrong all the time and that neither understood that there are good ways and bad ways to argue.

With Kim and Tony there was no middle ground. No compromise. No apologies. No attempts to solve the problem. The scenes were as bad as two children fighting and shouting, "It's your fault!" "My way!" "Shut up!" "Do it!" "That's stupid!"

One day Kim griped that such arguing left her excessively tired and depressed, and it just ruined her whole day. Tony countered by saying (with a smile), "It doesn't bother me much since I know I'm right." But he sensed the unhappiness that arguing caused and suggested they try just ignoring the problems. That idea lasted about three days before there was another emotional eruption.

At this point Kim noticed an article in the newspaper about a class at their junior college called "Conflict Resolution." Willing to try anything, they went and found that although others had similar problems, there were actual civilized techniques for handling disagreements. They learned problem-solving methods, and as a result, their married life became more calm and pleasant. Of course they still have quarrels, but now they know better what to do about them.

Some husbands and wives *never* learn what to do about quarrels. They accept these upsets as inevitable in their marriage relationship. However, *the inability to solve problems amicably is a Master Destroyer of marriages.* One divorced woman said, "We never took the time to really settle one single issue. We couldn't even agree to disagree—all of our communication was loud and rude, and each argument added another layer of hurt, another rift in our relationship. Finally, there was nothing worth saving."

Who wants to live in an environment of stress, turmoil, and frustration? Learning how to solve problems for *oneself* is essential for personal success and happiness. Learning how to solve problems *together* is essential for a strong and lasting marriage.

Partners should also face up to the fact that every disagreement doesn't require a villain and a victim. Some things just aren't worth the stress of a full-blown argument, and the same point can be made with a more gentle approach and a more gentle response.

It would have been much better if Kim had said, "I hoped you'd remember the dry-cleaning since I was planning to wear that dress to the party—but I'll find something else." With this response she puts the problem in perspective: the world will continue to revolve even though he forgot. And then Tony might have responded, "Gee, you're right, I do seem to be more forgetful lately, but I'll try to make myself a note next time. I'm really sorry about the dress."

The Fabulous 400 had both serious and humorous suggestions on how to end arguments. Just listen to these:

 **70 PUTTING FIRST THINGS FIRST** One couple say that an argument can take your focus off the important things. Remembering long-range goals helps to keep the marriage on an even keel. Long-range goals include a happy and enduring marriage so this couple remember to daily reaffirm their love, no matter what else is going on in their lives. Flexibility and mutual respect, plus the recognition of the true significance of their family, go a long way in peacefully settling their arguments.

71 THE DOG DECIDES Sometimes a decision just has to be made, and it is not earth-shaking which way it goes. So, let your dog decide! Standing or sitting in front of the dog, each spouse states his position. Then together, they say "Fido, choose." The first person Fido looks at wins the decision. The loser can't blame the spouse, and no one can really be angry with a sweet, intelligent dog. Sounds silly, but it works.

72 A GOOD MOTTO Often we find a gem of wisdom in a poem. Henry Lyte's words (used as both a poem and a hymn) make good sense. He says: "Slow to chide, and quick to bless." However, there are certainly occasions in a marriage where it gets reversed. It is so easy to quickly criticize! How nice it would be to start—and conclude—an argument with words of blessing or appreciation.

73 **DIVIDING, NOT MULTIPLYING**   Taking the time of two busy people to make a decision can be a waste of precious time. By dividing responsibilities and letting each person make certain decisions individually, you can save time. Of course there have to be some limits. The person in charge of car maintenance is not empowered to sell the car. The person in charge of social events isn't empowered to invite fifty friends for dinner. But, within reason, each person can act independently. Then, after a period of time, such as every three months, switch the responsibilities. This gives each partner opportunities to do things in his or her own special way, and also to appreciate what the other spouse has done.

74 **NOT NOW**   As you go out the door, or sit down for dinner, or put your head on your pillow for a good night's rest—these are not appropriate times for contentious conversation. With great kindness say, "I agree that this subject is important, so I want to give it thought. When could we sit down and discuss it?" Sometimes spur-of-the-moment disagreements aren't worth the time for talk later, but if the topic is important, jointly set the time for talk and then follow through.

75 **FAULTS AND HABITS**   Everyone has them, but many folks don't realize how some of their little idiosyncracies irritate others. Instead of constant nagging and criticism, try subtle reminding. One couple came up with a solution to his annoying fault of leaning on the table with arms and chest while eating, and her bad habit of being perpetually late. They decided on a signal, a silent signal, that would remind the other of these faults. They chose to pull on their own right earlobe as a cue to the other. At mealtime, she'd just look right at him and give the signal. He'd smile and comply by sitting back in his chair. When they were getting ready to go somewhere together, he'd give the signal that meant she'd better start preparations to leave. It worked far better than nagging.

76 **WHISPER**   One husband found a good way to diffuse shouting during a disagreement. Either spouse can announce: "Whisper!" It's quite difficult to sustain anger when you keep your voice very low (and the neighbors will appreciate your consideration, too)! He says that whispering often results in laughing, and the argument dissolves into hugs and apologies.

77 **I NEED** . . . .   Arguments arise when one spouse isn't getting needed support. After an unpleasant scene where one spouse makes demands, the other spouse often says, "Well, I didn't know you wanted that!" Be frank in your marriage. Speak up. Be explicit about what you need or want and request feedback. Putting your needs into words helps you to be more specific, and this verbalization helps you see the logic or irrelevance of your request.

78 **TICKLES**   One wife has a very simple solution to warding off a fight. "Sometimes when I notice that he's working himself into a snit over something, I just grab him and tickle him. Then in a moment, we talk about it." While this is not recommended for a disagreement at the office, it can certainly work at home. Do be careful about making light of another person's point of view. Still, it's worth trying on those occasions where a little tickling can break the anger spell.

79 **GO FOR A PRO**   When the strife in a marriage reaches a point where there seems to be no solution, it's time to get help. Often a third party can see right through the problem and suggest a variety of answers. We all need outside assistance at times, so don't be stubborn and refuse help. You may find a listening ear by calling on a parent, a good friend or neighbor, your clergy, a professional psychologist, or marriage counselor. There's no shame in recognizing that you can't do everything alone. It is the mature person who knows when to call for help.

THE POWER PLOY

The center of most arguments is power—who has it, who wants it, and how it is used. Just as children manipulate a parent's power for their own use, spouses use the power ploy between each other to get what they want. In many cases, they don't realize until too late that their misuse of power becomes the eye of the hurricane. These spouses don't want to lose control; and instead of sharing it, they grab control by arguing and wearing down the other party.

The clinical term for this condition is "unbalanced marriage": one partner dominating the other. Few unbalanced marriages last long. Research shows that the dominated spouse gradually loses the inclination to disagree and fight back, becoming so apathetic and in need of validation that the mind-set resembles senility. Soon the domineering spouse loses interest because there's no response from the other. When there is no confrontation left, the domineering spouse might move on to find the challenge of another spirit to break.

Many spouses (more often wives than husbands) just resign themselves to the other spouse's "taking charge" in most matters. Over the past centuries, the typical division has been that women were responsible for home and family, and that men were believed to excel in managing everything else.

But the balanced or egalitarian marriage is gradually gaining momentum. This is a marriage where the power is shared and shifted between the partners. There are no sex biases and the decisions are made on facts, rather than on emotional explosions.

The power of two, as opposed to the power of one, makes for the best and most long-lasting marriages. Each partner feels empowered to make decisions, to seek counsel, to debate a point of view without fear of the consequences. Ridicule and insults find no foothold in this kind of marriage.

UNHAPPY COUPLES

There is a definite difference between the way happy couples and unhappy couples handle their complaints. The unhappy ones criticize with sarcasm or jibes, always making the issues personal, and always on the attack. They truly believe that a good offense is the best defense.

Unhappy couples often use pouting, or silence, or even running away from the situation—much like a child who packs a sack and runs away from home, only to return when he gets hungry or cold.

There's a lot of help for unhappy couples if they'll only look for it. They can investigate the books in the "Self-help," "Psychology," or "Medical" sections of a library or bookstore. And, there is counseling, available through a hospital, physician, mental health association, the local United Way office, or a place of worship. It's essential that these woeful spouses don't simply give up. Though it may take time and trials to find what works, the end result can be worth it.

UNHAPPY COUPLES AND ABUSE

In a busy world with many pressures, instances of spousal abuse are increasing—and it goes both ways: verbal and physical by husband against wife, and vice versa. How can this happen in a civilized society? Why must disagreements go to such extremes?

Letting an unhappy state of marriage continue month after month and year after year is the first step toward the frustration that can lead to physically striking out at the other person. Of course, spousal abuse can be mental as well as physical, but the moment the relationship reaches the abusive level, lights should flash and bells should ring, and both partners should head directly for counseling without passing "Go."

It is vitally important that *immediate action* be taken and the violence brought into the open through counseling, in conversation with nearest friends and relatives, and if needed by filing police reports. Too often we see these steps taken too late. When it comes to a life or death matter (or the gray areas between), getting help or getting out are the only two options. There are proven methods taught in classes and self-help literature to read that can change this unhappy state into a more harmonious one.

Recent research shows that spousal abuse has the tendency to be passed on to the next generation, thus the importance of parents setting a good example for children. Children need to know that violence is not an acceptable response to disagreements.

Families need to be aware of the effect of television on relationships. What is seen on TV is perceived to be "the real world." So if women (or any group) are presented as objects of abuse or ridicule (dominated, useless, stupid, helpless), this sorry state becomes a self-fulfilling prophecy. Before finishing elementary school, television has shown the average child 8,000 murders and 100,000 other acts of violence. One in six youths between ages ten and seventeen has seen or knows someone who has been shot.

Unfortunately, research shows that spousal abuse goes hand-in-hand with the inability to communicate and thus resolve differences. Where there is no verbal connection, the response to disagreements is usually physical abuse. Spousal abuse has increased 56 percent in the last decade and child abuse is up 40 percent. Early help can change these figures, but not if spouses pretend that conflicts just don't exist.

HAPPY COUPLES

Happy couples do not withdraw from arguments, but they don't escalate them either. When one spouse withdraws from an argument (storming out of the room or sitting in sullen silence), the other has the tendency to increase the accusations in order to get a reaction. *He* wants to be heard! *She* wants her opinions acknowledged! Withdrawal from an argument by one partner can result in an escalation of resigned bitterness, or even worse—hatred by the other partner.

Happy couples realize that arguments are not necessarily a sign that the other partner is losing interest in the marriage. People who complain or disagree are often doing so in an attempt to make their marriage better. They do love their mate, but they don't like certain habits or attitudes. They have the techniques to make suggestions in a palatable way, to state a differing opinion, or to be insistent without being obnoxious. Thus, an important skill is *knowing how to disagree.*

WHAT CAUSES ARGUMENTS

My Fabulous 400 couples readily agree on what causes arguments. The big three are money, child rearing, and sex, followed by politics, religion, and differing ideas on leisure/social activities.

While some of these topics are common to all people, not just married couples, those living alone have the option to argue with friends and then go home and forget it. But when you live under the same roof with the person you're quarreling with, the argument can carry over into mealtime, leisure time, bedtime, and so forth, resulting in anger that lasts for many days to come.

So, it's imperative for couples to come to some agreement on these questions. Unfortunately these six problems are rarely settled permanently—different aspects of the same question pop up with some regularity. But when there is affection and good communication, *basic* agreements and concessions can be made so that there is a foundation for progress.

In a marriage, these six topics (and any others that cause arguments) need to be fully discussed and some conclusions reached. But remember, a marriage is always evolving and viewpoints change. While it is essential to make basic agreements, an open-ended dialogue is necessary to keep current on feelings and goals.

MONEY. What happens to our income? Does each partner have some discretionary funds to spend? How can we get out of debt? How can savings be put aside? A comprehensive discussion of money and marriage is in chapter 9.

CHILD REARING. Are children wanted? How many? How will they change our lifestyle? How can each parent be a positive influence? How can discipline be handled effectively? You'll find these answers and more in chapter 6.

SEX. What are the differing needs of each partner? What are the sexual "rights" of each partner? What can be done to avoid extramarital sex? Can we talk frankly about sex? You may wish to reread chapters 2 and 3.

POLITICS. Is it important to think alike? Will our differences negatively affect family life? While most couples feel that thinking alike is desirable, many say that it's good to have some differing opinions and to learn from each other.

RELIGION. On this question, most respondents favored a united front. Differing religions is a major cause of arguments. Separation on churchgoing days causes a rift in what can be an enriching experience. Many couples of differing faiths compromise by finding a church acceptable to both. Regular attendance at Sunday school and church services is an important bond for couples and family.

DIFFERING LEISURE/SOCIAL IDEAS. The use of free time for relaxation, social events, sports, classes, and hobbies is a major problem early on in many marriages. While younger couples battle to find time to "play" together, those married longer don't insist on as many dual activities. However, the important issue is to create and maintain a life beyond work and home. More on this essential element in a strong marriage can be found in chapter 7.

ARGUMENT ETIQUETTE

Argument etiquette is my term for knowing how to disagree in a mature and caring way. If you practice argument etiquette you may not have fewer disagreements, but they will be resolved in a more satisfying way. This form of etiquette includes these "don'ts":

- Don't say to the other person: "You're overreacting!" Keep your judgments to yourself.
- Don't say: "Leave me alone, I don't want to talk!" Instead, set a time to talk—sooner or later.
- Don't use children to communicate with—or get back at—your spouse. Speak directly to each other and leave the kids out of it.
- Don't use sex (or the lack of it) to manipulate your partner. Be fair, be loving.

- Don't use against your spouse something your spouse told you in confidence. A breach of trust is hard to repair.
- Don't say: "I don't have a problem, *you* have a problem." What bothers one spouse should concern both.
- Don't try to change your partner into some ideal person you imagine. Remember, we can't change our personality as easily as we can change our behavior.
- Don't accept only the outward appearance of an argument— search for the real issue that is sometimes hidden beneath the surface.
- Don't let arguments cause you to withdraw from each other for days at a time. Keep day-to-day living separate from the disagreement.
- Don't bring up divorce during a disagreement. Idle (or serious) threats will not solve the problem and can certainly escalate it.
- Don't ever let abuse be part of an argument. Remind yourself that you are a rational, thinking adult and you are dealing with the one you love.

So now you've had your etiquette lesson and you are ready for more ideas to quell quarrels and defuse disagreements.

 **80** **WHOSE WAY?** The question isn't about settling a problem *my* way, or *his* way, or *her* way. The question is how to find the *right* way. And often there is more than one right method. You'll also find that a wrong solution at one particular time is the right solution at another time. Don't let mere personality influence your decision by attaching the problem or solution to one person or the other. Keep looking for the right way.

81 **TODDLER TACTICS** Don't revert to childhood and use toddler ploys to get your way. Silence, pouting, or throwing things is not a mature way to solve problems. These scream for "My way, no-matter-what." Each partner needs to grow up and realize that reason takes precedence over emotional outbursts. Should a partner try toddler tactics, quietly suggest that settling the disagreement be postponed to a time when *both* participants are feeling adult enough to handle it.

82 I'M So MAD!
Getting furious isn't a healthy way to solve problems. Find out what calms you down so that the ensuing conversation is tranquil and rational. It could be a walk around the block, relaxing in a chair, or taking a warm shower. Those folks who have to physically work off the anger may choose to beat a pillow on the bed, rip yesterday's newspaper into strips, or slam a ball against the garage door. Whatever you choose, do it before you say or do something you'll regret later.

83 No POINTING
Shaking fingers may be acceptable when correcting a toddler or a pet, but it's a no-no between spouses. Pointing is a form of attack and indicates that the person you're pointing at has done something terribly wrong. "You" accusations are meant to hurt in order to correct, and hurting rarely brings positive results. In arguing, avoid pointing and pointed comments that begin with "you" ("You lost the key"; "You were late again"; "You spent too much money"). Rather than focus on your so-called opponent, focus on yourself. Tell how the action made you feel ("I feel sad because the vase is broken"; "I was hurt when you didn't come"; "I'm confused by what happened"). These "I" statements are more likely to get the receptive attention of the spouse than the "you" accusations.

84 I'M SORRY
Those are hard words to say and at times when we feel completely justi-

fied in our actions, we may not wish to apologize for what we did. But, you can smooth the troubled waters by being sorry for the *results* of your actions. "I'm sorry that what I did upset you." "I'm sorry my words made you sad." "I'm sorry that we can't agree." "I'm sorry about this problem, but I still love you."

HOW PROBLEMS ARE SOLVED

Before a damaging quarrel or power play can get started, the disagreement can be derailed in many ways. The Fabulous 400 shared their views on the best and worst ways of staving off or settling disagreements. These were their suggestions:

1. Discuss the problem and possible solutions, then make a plan together. (Over 73 percent chose this method, sometimes utilizing expert advice.)
2. Agree to a compromise. (9 percent)
3. Simply give in to the other. (8 percent)
4. One partner insists on his/her own way. (5 percent)
5. Ignore the problem. (3 percent)
6. Quietly wait, pray about, or forget the issue. (2 percent)

In strong long-term marriages, actively seeking a solution was an overwhelming response. One husband in my study said, "With each passing year of our twenty-six-year marriage, we disagree less. And that doesn't mean we give up our own ideas, it means that we are finding mutually agreeable ways to accomplish our aims."

Of course, problem solving is the best answer, but how does it work? It's important to isolate the issue as soon as it arises, although when tempers are hot, a cooling off period is wise. Set a time to talk about the issue, each party agreeing to think about it prior to the discussion. Prior to the discussion, each partner needs to honestly analyze the complaint to see if it is justified.

Pick a time, free from outside disturbances, a time that is open-ended. Agree on some simple rules: no shouting, no name calling, no accusations—whatever is apt to cause either of you to blow a gasket.

It may be helpful to have paper and pencil handy, first to write down what the problem is (we're spending more than we're earning, there's no time for us to be together, the kids are sassy and making us irritable, you don't help me enough). Then write down all the possible solutions, no matter how silly or improbable they seem. Sometimes a wild notion will lead to a very practical idea. In every problem-solving discussion, try to find some area of agreement, no matter how small. Then build on that.

Next, carefully discuss *all* the solutions. Together, rate them in order of preference and feasibility. Choose one conclusion to implement over a certain period of time (a week, a month) with the understanding that if the idea is given a fair test and it doesn't work, another means of settlement will be tried.

Finally, determine how to implement the chosen solution. Define the responsibility of each partner. Discuss how the solution can be given the best chance to succeed. Let there be no fuzziness about the solution and its implementation, for halfhearted support could lead to an early breakup of the solution followed by another argument.

Sometimes the "complaint" is settled, yet there is lingering hostility. In such cases the "complaint" may have been a cover-up for the real problem and there needs to be the follow-up question: "Is something else bothering you?"

Using this somewhat time-consuming method for resolving arguments will result in both successes and failures. And, on some occasions, one partner may not wish to take this time, but rather be accommodating and quickly compromise or give in. Even this is a solution that can work.

However, making a concession is wise only when the partner giving in doesn't have strong feelings on the issue. Giving in and then harboring hurt feelings is definitely harmful to the relationship. This "injured" partner may start a tally of his/her concessions to use against the spouse at a later time.

The Fabulous 400 found most arguments were easy to avert or settle. They were aware of the damage caused by losing an argument, rather than by settling it amicably. When they outright lost an argument, they used these words to describe their feelings: *hurt, bitter, depressed, impatient, trapped, frustrated, angry, suffocated,* and *dominated.* When they solved a problem together (which happened most of the time), they said they felt *elated, calm, hopeful, victorious, loving, successful, intelligent,* and *happy.* If arguing can leave one as upset as the first list indicates, it's definitely better to take the time needed to solve the problem and enjoy the good feelings of the second list.

Here are some additional ideas:

85 **SETTING LIMITS** Arguments have the bad habit of flowing from one subject to another. A participant may erroneously think: "As long as we're discussing who caused the dent in the fender, I'll also throw in a few comments on his snoring." Gently insist on one topic at a time. If you've decided to settle a problem, settle that one problem before going on to another. You make little progress when you are talking on one subject and your spouse is challenging you on another front.

86 **LET'S VOTE ON IT** A very democratic family uses voting as a way to settle some problems. They call a family meeting and each person gets to state his or her views on the subject. A number of acceptable solutions are then written down and a vote is taken. If it's a very volatile issue, the vote is secret. Using this method, they've solved problems about bed and curfew times, spending money, eating less junk food, where to go camping, room cleanliness, and honesty at school. Democracy does work!

87 **KING-SIZED SOLUTION** A couple with fifty years of marriage experience has a unique way of simmering down arguments. When things start to get out of hand, one leads the other to the bedroom. There, stretched out next to each other on their king-sized bed, they find that they can usually calmly resolve the problem. Returning to the scene of so many delightful encounters, they find that physical closeness can result in mental closeness.

88 **WHAT IF . . .?** When a solution seems elusive, or when discussion leads to quarreling, consider the "what ifs." What if my husband never learns to pick up his clothes off the floor? What if my wife never learns to cook? What if we never make any friends? What if we go deeper into debt? The answer to such questions is termed the "worst scenario." Sometimes you can just live with a problem if the "worst scenario" isn't too bad. At other times, you'll realize how disastrous the "worst scenario" is and work all the harder to remedy the problem.

89 **JUST THE FACTS** Too many arguments begin because of misunderstandings. Make sure *each of you* knows the facts in the situation that is causing the argument. You may find instant agreement when you're both on the same wavelength.

90 **BEFORE THE SUN SETS** A wise minister paraphrased the Bible verse in Ephesians 4:26 and said, "Never let the sun set on your anger." While you may not settle the question that caused the anger, *settle the anger* with thoughts and gestures of your love for one another. Don't go to bed mad! The new day may bring better ideas for a solution.

91 **AFTERWARD**   When the disagreement is over, it's over. Unless absolutely necessary, don't bring up the argument ever again. This may not be easy, but each time you rehearse it, you make it more of an element in your marriage. Forget it happened. Soon you'll think it never did happen.

• • •

While Kim and Tony had to take a conflict resolution course to learn how to amicably solve their disagreements, many couples with strong marriages find solutions by sticking to reason and "argument etiquette." This is made easier when you remember that the one you're arguing with is the one you love.

When baby makes three

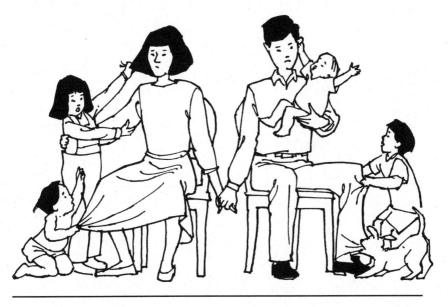

"But Daddy said I could!" whined Melissa. In her motherly fashion, Cecile snapped back, "You'd already asked me and I had said you couldn't. Now, since you wheedled your father's OK, I guess you're going to that stupid sleep-out at the park!" Melissa ducked out of the kitchen, having won another skirmish.

When Rico came into the kitchen, he could tell by looking at his wife that something was wrong. "I didn't know you'd told her she couldn't go," he said. Cecile answered angrily, "The kids know you're the patsy, they can get you to say yes to anything." He argued back, "Well, I didn't think there was anything wrong in sleeping out at the park with the group. My mom let me do it when I was a kid."

"Your mom," Cecile shot back, "didn't know beans about raising kids. Besides, you were a teenager aeons ago and it's different these days."

Now Rico was getting angry. "Lay off my mom! Your parents actually encouraged your brothers to be good-for-nothing loafers."

Melissa, who'd been listening at the kitchen door, found her brother in the living room and smugly announced, "They're at it again."

T he marriage years when children are at home are the most stressful, and consequently many marriages split up over different approaches to childrearing. Second marriages with blended families create additional problems. And some marriages don't work because of strife with parents and in-laws. Even after youngsters have left home, they can be disruptive to their parents' relationship. Although married couples with children now make up only 26 percent of U.S. households (down from almost 50 percent a generation ago, according to the Bureau of the Census), many emerging conditions have made parenting more difficult and more apt to cause rifts in a family.

Divorce with consequent single parenting, neighborhood crime, the increase of abuse within the family, the overwhelming effect of television violence, permissive and immoral behavior, earlier and inappropriate sexual activity, overworked career mothers, and fathers who work two jobs—all these influences can add worry and tension to the married-with-children years. If a marriage is going to break up, these are the years when it's most apt to happen.

Of all the problems that strain a family, those involving the disciplining and educating of children are among the biggest. This is followed by parents and in-laws interfering in both the marriage and child care.

One husband put it this way: "If our family of four could live on a desert island away from the rest of the world, we'd be as happy as fleas on a sheepdog." Short of becoming fleas, how can we live in harmony with children, grandchildren, parents and society in general?

The Fabulous 400 in my study were almost unanimous in recommending that early in their marriage parents come to a meeting of the minds on child rearing. Unity of purpose and method makes for more successful and contented parenting. This is one topic that shouldn't wait until the children are out of control. The dialogue must start before children are born and then it must continue for several decades.

Marriage and family create other situations that can bring strife. When a couple marry, they create a new relationship with their parents and in-laws. Each generation needs to be careful not to overstep the bounds of this relationship and become meddlesome or nagging. For the older folks, the years of correction and guidance are over and the two generations now (hopefully) become more like friends. Only when opinions are requested should parents step back into the former guidance mode. And once a suggestion is given, parents should not interfere any further unless asked. This is sometimes hard! But the best lessons are often learned through the sufferings of the trial and error method.

Most married couples feel satisfied and in control when they have solved with each other the problems of finance or curbing bad habits or finding time for communication. Here, the challenge is just between husband and wife. But sometimes couples feel out of control in working out the problems that arise with children because kids can be both charming and manipulative, sidetracking the parents' goals. Now the problems no longer involve just two, but rather three or four. And the answers are many-faceted and more difficult to come by.

Don't let children—the biggest blessing of marriage—be the cause of such strife that the outcome is the dissolution of the marriage! Many researchers find that striving to save a marriage is usually better than divorcing and remarrying, thus upsetting the lives of parents and children. Whatever the problems were in the first marriage often reappear the second time around, so it can be easier to stay and strive for a good solution.

WHY CHILDREN CAN UPSET MARRIAGES

Raising a child is manifestly different from growing roses or opening a branch office. There is something different going on each day. Just when parents think they've mastered one challenge, another pops up to confound and exhaust them. Many disagreements between spouses are caused by the frustrating things kids do.

Parents need to see that a loving but firm hand is the best way to raise responsible and happy children. Too many parents let the child become the center of attention. They think that what makes the child happy is all-important—and they, as parents, don't count. Actually, the family unit, not the child, should be the center of attention. *What makes the entire family happy and productive is most important.*

In our concern for our children, we have been brainwashed into thinking that making children feel good about themselves no matter what leads to self-esteem. What a disservice to children to let them feel grand about doing poor or mediocre work when they are capable of something greater! When they later find out how you lied to inflate their achievements, they might be depressed and frustrated. And, they will have lost confidence in you.

With teen suicide wrecking so many families because youngsters don't think their lives are worth anything, it is imperative that parents teach kids how valuable they are, as well as the wide range of unique possibilities that life offers.

An integral part of building self-worth comes from the recognition of less-than-perfect actions. The responsible parent both encourages and corrects. One father uses the phrase, "What you have done is not worthy of you."

If we are to raise children to recognize their true potential, we should not be "giving" them self-esteem. It cannot be given; it can only be learned and earned. So, our aim as caring parents is to give youngsters many occasions and activities that let them accumulate self-worth. We do this through reason, democracy, education, and providing daily opportunities for kids to make decisions to do the right (or wrong) thing and reap the rewards or punishments. Children raised in this manner will not give their parent pain. They will be assets to the parents' marriage, making it even stronger than it was before the child or children became part of the family.

Then comes the day when the last fledgling leaves the nest. When this happens, many couples find that they have buried the troublesome parts of their marriage under the umbrella of all-consuming child-rearing. Suddenly a twosome again, they find they have trouble relating to each other and having a meaningful and enjoyable life together. This points to the need for proper balance between parent and child and between parent and parent *all through the marriage.*

At the same time there can be a feeling of loss when the nest is empty. A parent realizes a relinquishment of power—the child is now making decisions alone. It soothes the separation to keep communication alive, to make visits, but most important to get on with your own life.

So that a marriage doesn't self-destruct because of children, it's necessary to recognize the ways that youngsters—and other relatives—can innocently or purposefully cause strife. Having recognized these challenges, you are ready to triumph over them.

HARMONY WITHIN THE FAMILY

Here are some ideas to help parents in the all-important area of child discipline. As you know, disagreements over child rearing is another one of the Master Destroyers of marriage.

UNITED WE STAND   While parents can have minor differences in some child-rearing concepts, they must be united on discipline and family rules. One parent mustn't be the never-bending ogre while the other is the wishy-washy disciplinarian. Differences in the application of corrective measures should be worked out between the parents in advance of need and without the child present. The child needs to know that both parents believe in the importance of just, even-handed discipline.

No Two Opinions   Make it clear to youngsters that the answer they get from one parent is the one and only answer. Do not permit a child to secretly ask the same question of the other parent in hopes of getting a more favorable response. If a child breaks this rule, the more strict answer of the two will apply. This doesn't mean that a child can't state his case to the other parent, but he should be sure to inform that parent of the first parent's decision. Don't let this kind of manipulation by kids cause husband/wife arguments.

TAKING TURNS   When one parent—mother or father—is in full charge of the children during the weekdays, the other parent can take command for most of the weekend—starting with Friday evening. It is always pleasant to have some time off from parental guidance and this also gives the other parent an opportunity for interaction with the youngsters.

No MATTER WHAT   Discipline is the least-liked of parental duties. When possible, point out to kids the importance of the corrective measures you are using, and also that discipline is necessary because of your love for the child. Be sure to tell youngsters that you love them "no matter what." Children need to know that they are important to their parents, not just a bother. Tell them often how happy you are that they are adding good times to your marriage.

TRUE TO YOUR WORD Honesty in a parent/child relationship is just as important as in a husband/wife relationship. If you announce to a youngster the consequences for breaking a rule, see that you follow through. Rarely should you default on your word and if that happens, be sure to explain why you backed off. Youngsters need parameters in which to live. Definite rules, rewards, and punishments give them a feeling of safety through staying within the boundaries their parents have set. Put simply, say what you mean, and mean what you say!

A PARENT'S CHANGING ROLE

As youngsters grow up to adulthood, mothers—and some fathers—experience a startling change in their lives. Many have moved from a career into motherhood, or combined motherhood and career, and then back to a full-time career again, or to a life of leisure and service. While men, who have traditionally been less involved with home and children, may handle the changes more easily, a woman often finds that these shifts have clouded her vision of what a marriage should be. She is no longer vitally needed at home, in charge of the lives of children, or the expediter of household affairs. Feelings of unfulfillment, perhaps low self-worth, or uselessness can set in. A caring spouse and a strong husband/wife bond is the best defense as women readjust their goals for life. There *is* life after children!

98 **EMPTY NEST**   When kids leave home for college and you are still paying their way, remember that you have certain rights—rights you need to discuss *before* the youngster is accepted at the school. Too many parents are forced to near-bankruptcy by kids who feel they are "owed" an expensive college education. You'll want to talk about educational performance (yes, you will require seeing their grades), spending money and abiding by a livable budget, handling emergencies, the use of alcohol or drugs, insurance coverage, sound eating habits as opposed to health-threatening junk food diets, keeping in touch (low cost evening phone service), planned visits (super-saver airfares and ride sharing), and making new friends. Don't let these years be the beginning of estrangement between you and your youngster. Set the rules up front. And remember, this is the start of a wonderful new life for just you and your spouse.

99 **"YOU'RE NOT MY MOM!"**   Stepparenting can wreck a marriage if the spouses are not united on how the new family will operate. When youngsters resent a new stepparent, they have amazing power to cause distress, especially since the stepparent often feels threatened by comparison with the birth parent. *Early on*, spouses should discuss the situation, and then explain to the youngsters who is in charge, and what the rules, rewards, and punishments will be. One stepmother had a good response to the child's shouted, "You're not my mom!" She quietly said, "I know that, but I'm your dad's wife, so I'm the one who is in charge in this house." Stepparents should work extra hard to be supportive of each other so that the stepchildren realize that it's of no advantage to try to break up the marriage.

HARMONY WITH PARENTS AND IN-LAWS

While an overwhelming percentage of couples in the survey described their relationships with parents and in-laws as pleasant, the Fabulous 400 were quick to share their methods for keeping the peace. For those who found their relatives unpleasant, the answer was minimal contact—how unfortunate for both sides! As one husband said, "After all, I married my wife, not her parents!"

Problem parents and in-laws were described with these words: *meddlesome, bossy, boring, selfish, manipulative, devious, vulgar, fault-finding, divisive, hateful, intolerant, money-grabbing, alcoholic, sneaky, judgmental, lying, competitive,* and *unkind.* With a list like that, it is no wonder that a married couple would opt for limited contact!

Don't let parents and in-laws spoil your marriage! The moment you're introduced to the in-laws, start to build a satisfying relationship. When there are differences of opinion, try to work them out as quickly as possible. This is especially important when there are children, since the child/grandparent connection can be beneficial to all three generations. An appreciation and love for both sets of grandparents can be a blessing to youngsters and one more thread in the fabric of a strong marriage.

These ideas may help to maintain a loving bond between grandparents, parents, and their children.

SPEAK NO EVIL ⭕⭕ **100** When a parent or in-law starts to be openly critical of a husband or wife, nip this bad habit in the bud. (Rarely is it a subject that the spouse is unaware of. Rarely is it meant in a so-called helpful way.) Spouses should be supportive of each other and not take any part in this mean exchange, other than to stop it. Letting it continue can signal agreement, and this puts a rift in the marriage. It is up to each spouse to tell his or her own parents in no uncertain terms that criticism will not be tolerated. Stop it with lines like, "I know you feel that way, but we can handle the situation." "We appreciate your concern, but just try to be supportive." "This really is none of your business, so let's not talk about it."

101 SECRET CRITICISM   What happens when parents don't criticize openly but secretly bad-mouth the person their own child married? For example, a mother criticizes a daughter-in-law when the daughter-in-law is absent from the conversation. One husband handled it by saying to his mother, "Will you say that to her face? If not, let's drop the subject." Another said, "This is a private matter between my wife and me, so let's talk about something else." There should be no secrets; when the secret is later discovered, it will surely cause hurt feelings and a major argument between the couple. A husband or wife's first allegiance is to the other partner.

102 COMPARING GRANDCHILDREN   Grandparents should learn not to compare their grandchildren but rather appreciate the unique individuality of each. While they can occasionally make suggestions for improvement, they should not comment on how one child is superior to another. Sometimes when your parent rants about the shortcomings of your child, your parent is subtly criticizing your mate. Don't listen to such garbage. Change the subject, and if that doesn't work, politely excuse yourself and walk out of the room. It is easy to criticize youngsters that you don't know well or see often. Parents should share with grandparents good things about their grandchildren so that grandparents will have something positive to talk about.

INTERFERING IN CHILD REARING

103 When grandparents are asked to care for grandchildren, they should be instructed in the family rules, activities that are acceptable, the approved method of discipline, and they should follow these parameters unless there is an overwhelming reason to do something else. Unless grandparents are in charge of grandchildren on a regular basis, they should not take over the duties of the parents, but rather establish a relationship of love, companionship, and respect with the youngsters.

THE IMPORTANCE OF GRANDPARENTS

104 Since as many grandparents feel out of touch with the younger generation, parents should help these still vital people feel important to the lives of their grandchildren. Keep the lines of communication open through family get-togethers, sharing of photos, phone calls, cassette messages sent across the miles, and regular remembrances. It's a shame to waste the wonderful assets of a grandparent's knowledge and love.

ONE THING AT A TIME

105 Calm grandparents' fears by letting them know that you are working on the shortcomings of your children. But explain to them that you are working on one thing at a time (obedience, toilet training, study habits, sharing) and that you wish them to be supportive of that one idea and not confuse the issue by bringing up many unrelated suggestions. Grandparents often have the habit of making a slew of recommendations at one time. For example, if a child is learning good table manners and the grandparents are present at a meal, they shouldn't nag and note every little failure or infraction, but rather set a good example and compliment even small successes.

106 **FAMILY HISTORY**   Assign grandparents the job of sharing family history through photos, trips to old neighborhoods, and stories of the old days. Encourage grandparents to tell grandchildren stories about you (the child's parent) when you were young. Your kids will love to hear some of your growing-up antics. Seeing you in this new context brings you closer together.

107 **TALENT SHOW**   Many kids don't realize how smart their grandparents are. Encourage conversation and questions about work, favorite sports, and special talents. Let a grandparent take over the sharing of a special talent with a grandchild—fishing, knitting, bowling, model making, whistling, bugle blowing, dancing, making marionettes, home repairs, painting, playing the piano, and so forth. While the grandparents are having fun working and playing with the grandkids, you'll reap extra time to spend with your spouse.

108 **IF ALL ELSE FAILS**   One husband reported that he found it impossible to keep peace between his wife and his mother. No amount of reasoning could stop the bickering that spoiled most family get-togethers. The only time they were even slightly civil was at Thanksgiving and Christmas when other relatives were present. Finally, with his wife's encouragement, the husband made a plan to see his mother separately, taking her out for supper and conversation one weekday evening twice a month. She loved the special attention! While this isn't an ideal solution, the couple felt it worked best for them.

109 **LOOKING FOR GOOD** Somewhere, buried inside grandparents or in-laws who seem to be disagreeable, are qualities that can be appreciated, if they can be uncovered. One wife found that it helped to actually write these down and relay them to her husband. Occasionally he mentioned them to his parents, who were happy to hear that their daughter-in-law noticed something special about them. The wife was pleased with her ability to hold her tongue and thought to herself, "They have to be good people; after all, they gave me a great husband."

110 **CHOOSE YOUR ENVIRONMENT** The usual weekly dinner at the grandparents' house can be a boring event for the kids, as well as stressful for the spouses if one partner sides with the children in not wanting to go. Put variety into your family get-togethers. Have a picnic in a park, attend a sports event or a play, let everyone make cookies together, sit outside in the dark and have the grandparents relate a favorite scary story. Don't be routine about three-generation activities. Variety is truly the spice of life together.

111 **LIVING TOGETHER** When parents and their married children must live together, it can mean rough weather ahead. Few families can ride out the storms of differing habits, divided home management, interference in child rearing, and combined financial arrangements. Only one couple in my study thought that living with parents was a good idea. But, if there is no other way (or if you truly believe it will benefit your marriage rather than tear it apart), go about joining the households in a businesslike way. Write down exactly what each expects of the other in both living and financial arrangements. Set a date (three to six months ahead) to renegotiate the arrangement.

HARMONY WITH GROWN-UP CHILDREN

When kids leave home for college or career, they usually believe that they no longer need any parenting. Yet even though they are supposedly launched on their own, they can have a negative impact on the two of you. Many couples have learned the hard way that grown-up kids can bring stress and grief to their parents' marriage. These ideas may serve as warnings and solutions.

112 **BORROWING MONEY**   Money is the biggest problem between parents and grown children and consequently between parent and parent. After all, you don't want your children to starve, or live in a roach-infested apartment, or dress so shabbily that they can't land a job! So, you decide to give in to their request for funds. First, tell these grown-up kids that you don't enjoy being involved in their finances since it changes the parent/child relationship. Then, if you must lend money, do it in a businesslike way with a written note that includes the repayment schedule and signatures of each spouse (the parents' and the youngsters') so that everyone knows the details of the arrangement. Don't lend more than you can afford to lose. Be sure that you are equitable between children, not giving more money to one than another. Make it clear to the one who constantly borrows that he is using up part of the money he might receive in the ensuing years.

113 **RETURNING HOME**   Nowadays, more young people are returning home to live with their parents—both before and after marriage—and these parents are shocked at how different their lives become when they are no longer a happy twosome. The clue to making this living arrangement work is to spell out what you require of the kids before the move is made. Show how it will be very different from the days of carefree childhood. Questions to settle include: how much rent to pay (including utilities), payment for a proper share of the food, use and care of common areas and share of house-keeping duties, entertaining, music and noise that could be disturbing, and the care and discipline of any children. (Often when the youngster finds out what parents expect, they'll find a way to live on their own.) In the case of a young adult out of work, set requirements for actively seeking interviews and taking a temporary job in the interim. Letting adult children return home can result in a hotbed of problems that strain a marriage. If it must happen, put a time limit on the duration, say three months. Then, before continuing, have a frank conversation about the arrangement and see how it can be improved for all parties.

114 **GIVING ADVICE** Married couples are often relieved when the years of day-to-day parenting are over. Surprise! Yes, while some grown-up youngsters may appear to have divorced themselves from their parents, others still need advice. Of course you care deeply about the person you knew as baby and teen, but you no longer need to be forced into responsibility for this adult's decisions. When you are asked for advice, it may be that your young adult just wants a listening ear. Use lines like: "Tell me all about it." "I'm sure you'll know what to do." "Your education/expertise will lead you to the right answer." Suggest many options but don't be forced into drawing conclusions that young adults need to make on their own. Don't deprive your youngster of the ability to make decisions—that's part of growing up.

KEEPING IN TOUCH   Regular communication is the key to a continuing good relationship. When youngsters first leave home, the communication may be daily or weekly. When these young adults establish their own homes, weekly or every other week is ideal. Less frequent communication becomes cursory and can lead to estrangement. In addition to phone calls, write letters, send greeting cards, and arrange get-togethers and trips—all good ways of keeping in touch.

SPECIAL OCCASIONS   The memorable occasions of youth—birthdays, anniversaries, Christmas, Thanksgiving, and other holidays—are important ones for a family to celebrate together throughout the years. Building memories doesn't end when a child leaves home—actually some of the best memories are still to come. However, when a youngster marries, understand that there are now in-laws who want their share of holiday company, too, so be gracious and change off each year. Don't hog these special occasions by insisting on your way at your house. And when the youngsters aren't going to be with you, do something special as a twosome. When invited to the younger generation's homes, let them be organizers and hosts and you may gain some new ideas.

HARMONY WITHIN THE WIDER CIRCLE OF FAMILY

Good memories can result from association with the extended family that includes aunts, uncles, cousins, and so forth. These relationships give depth to a marriage and strengthen its bonds through the years. Use the following ideas to encourage memorable togetherness.

ROUND-ROBINS Start a round-robin **117** style letter to go to all relatives. Include with the letter a list of the order in which the letter is to go. You may want to include everyone's current address the first time. Suggest that each person read the letters and add a new one of his own within two weeks. Write briefly but include interesting happenings, questions, clippings of interest, and photos. See how long it takes for the letter to make the rounds and come back to you. Then, remove your old letter, write a new one, pack it up with the accumulated letters and send it off once more.

CALL-OF-THE-MONTH Make a list of **118** all the relatives and near-relatives that you don't see very often. With input from your own family on whom to call, telephone one each month. Before making the call, bring your family up-to-date on the one you're calling so everyone can participate. You don't need to talk for long, but let youngsters share some of their own news, too. After the call, discuss what each one learned.

THE REUNION Plan well ahead for **119** an informal get-together of the entire clan. Choose a weekend at least six months in advance and select a place such as a park or campground. Make an agenda for a two- or three-day event. Suggest nearby inexpensive overnight accommodations. Arrange for participants to bring old photos, games, and assign foods for the first potluck meal. Give prizes for the oldest and youngest attending, the one coming the farthest, and so forth. Plan excursions and games. Have a mock re-marriage ceremony for all the couples to renew their vows.

ADOPT A RELATIVE   If you're short of
⊙⊙ **120** relatives, consider "adopting" a friend or
neighbor whose company your family
enjoys. Treat this person with the same interest and affection
that you would a beloved blood relative. This association can
enhance your youngster's growing-up years, but also provide
you and your spouse with a new close friend. You'll find more
about the importance of friends in chapter 7.

FINDING THE TIME TO BE BOTH SPOUSE AND PARENT

Almost one-half of the parents in our survey felt that they
had insufficient time to interact with their children. And over
95 percent of those who felt they had too little time to build
the parent/child relationship were men. While older respondents regretted this lost time, the younger ones were diligent
in their plans to carve out and maintain this important interaction.

Today there is a very positive swing toward fathers being
equally involved in parenting. This shared experience is so
important to a strong marriage, because it adds one more
bond between husband and wife. Here are some ideas to pro-
mote this togetherness.

TWO THINGS AT ONCE   Make the
⊙⊙ **121** most of work time by combining it with
family-oriented activities. Let a child read
a book to you as you fold the laundry or wash the car. Help
with practice for a spelling test as you make supper. Play
games during TV commercials. Listen to and talk about music
during dinner. Use car-time for conversation and games. When
you're going out and will be parted from your child, let the
child be your maid or valet and help you dress. While giving a
child undivided attention is great, doing two things at once
can be fun, as well as a subtle example to the kids.

MANY HANDS Kids' help around the house is educational for them and saves you time that you can spend with your mate. Depending on a child's age, assign chores such as emptying wastebaskets, weeding and garden care, dusting and vacuuming, folding laundry, doing dishes or loading/unloading the dishwasher, setting the table, caring for a pet, sharpening pencils, preparing school lunches, or making part of dinner. Depending on how many children you have, assign a preschooler about ten minutes of "helps" each day, a grade schooler about thirty minutes of work, and teens about forty-five minutes per day. For added togetherness, do some of the jobs with your youngster.

PLAN AHEAD Don't waste precious weekend free time wondering what to do together. Starting on Monday, have a brainstorming session at the dinner table. Make plans for a date with your spouse plus an all-family activity that might occasionally include friends. Spend a specified amount of time on Saturday morning doing necessary home chores and errands. Then, go for the fun. Of course you'll want to leave room for spontaneous suggestions for activities, but always have an enjoyable family event to look forward to each week.

A PLACE FOR PARENTING In the kitchen or family room, have your parenting headquarters. You can read more about this in chapter 8; however, a desk with drawers and a bulletin board with calendar are parenting essentials. Use the drawers for files on each child (health records, grades, awards), guarantees and warranties on things in the house, gift ideas, recipes and entertaining lists, travel clippings, and important papers. Let one drawer be for memorabilia—all those kid drawings you can't toss out, school and sport programs, birthday cards, and so forth. Save time by posting these lists on the bulletin board: chores, repairs, groceries, phone numbers of friends, and whom to call for emergencies. Insist on a weekly update of the calendar so that family events don't conflict and so you can carve out time to be with your spouse. Being efficient will give you extra togetherness time.

125 **TAKE FIVE**   Get up five minutes ahead of everyone else in the family. Sit in a cozy place and think about the day. Let ideas just come to you. Be grateful for good things that have happened. If you feel inclined, pray. Then start the morning routine. You may be amazed to find that having spent five minutes on your own mental well-being, the day ahead goes more efficiently and more pleasantly.

126 **THE YEARS GO BY**   When you're busy and inclined to brush off youngsters' requests and questions, remind yourself that there will come a time when the kids are no longer under the roof. As pleasant as that may sound now, invest in the future of your family by taking a focused interest in today. Settle minor problems before they grow into big problems. Along with your spouse, keep a family journal and write about something good that happened during the day or week.

•   •   •

Cecile and Rico, whose story opened this chapter, finally got their priorities straight, and in many ways their marriage as well as their relationship with the kids has improved. They finally realized that a united front in disciplining children was important, and that they, as parents, had rights. When they exercised these rights, the result was increased satisfaction for the entire family.

⊙⊙ 127 THE PARENTS' BILL OF RIGHTS

To keep your marriage and your family strong,
here is your own Bill of Rights.

💜 *The right to enjoy the parenting years because you keep well informed on your child's changing interests and needs.*

💜 *The right to have ample time for your own personal activities such as sports, hobbies, and classes.*

💜 *The right to a social life free from children, just as they have the right to playtime without your constant presence.*

💜 *The right to feel good about saying no to a child when the request is not in keeping with your rules or values.*

💜 *The right to have respect from children, the same respect you give to them, your spouse, family, and friends.*

💜 *The right to tell the truth and be told the truth.*

💜 *The right to laugh at yourself and find joy in both work and play.*

💜 *The right to have time for affection, to love your spouse, and be loved in return.*

💜 *The right to share your burdens with and be comforted by God who lovingly cares for all his children.*

💜 *The right to life, liberty, and the pursuit of happiness with the ones you love.*

Marriage is supposed to be fun?

"It was great being single," Ralph admitted rather sheepishly, "but I wouldn't trade our twenty years of marriage for anything."

Barb agreed, but with one reservation: "We had so much fun in those early years; every day was a special day. It isn't that we aren't getting along now—the kids are almost grown, we have a house and good jobs— but somehow the fun just isn't there anymore."

"I hope we aren't just getting old!" said Ralph with a twinkle.

Barb quickly answered, "Not us, we're going to see what we can do to bring back those happy days."

Those happy days shouldn't end with marriage! Neither should the increasing responsibilities of home, family, and work mean the end of fun. Good times and marriage go hand in hand.

When single, most people put equal importance on their job and their social life. Then, when they find the person they'd like to marry, social times assume even greater importance. Dating the one you love is such fun! Next comes the excitement of the wedding and a new life as a twosome.

This is when the balance begins to shift. The responsibility of earning a living takes on greater importance and your job becomes a focus, along with the needs of your spouse. If children soon follow, and also the purchase of a home, earning an income to pay for these becomes imperative. At this point, responsibilities and happiness juggle for top position. So, "having fun" gets pushed further down the priority list. But you *can* be both responsible and happy—those important elements of a marriage should be a copartnership.

Unfortunately many couples don't regain a work/play balance in their lives until the children are almost grown. This lack of enjoyable memory-building activities can result in a relationship built mainly on knocking out the work of day-to-day living. While work may be an admirable aim, it does little to increase the bond between husband and wife. It often becomes a barrier.

The result is that sometimes a spouse looks outside the relationship to find the happiness that marriage should bring. Master Destroyers of marital bliss include escaping to the world of television, hanging out with buddies to the exclusion of the spouse, being totally focused on children to the exclusion of each other, even having an affair—which all lead the participant into thinking that these time fillers are justifiable in an otherwise work-filled life.

There is no reason why the busiest years of marriage shouldn't also be

the most joyful. The Fabulous 400 couples in my study empha-
sized the importance of a life beyond the walls of the office or
home. "You have to carve out the time—make your fun times
just as important as your other appointments," said one husband of twenty-five years. His wife responded, "And, you have
to find satisfaction in the little things you do each day. I think
this is easier for women than for men."

While men are more inclined to search for new highs,
research shows that women are usually more content, happier, with everyday married life. One psychologist says that this
is a throwback to prehistoric times when men had plenty of
excitement in the chase for food and the defending of the
home. Whether this is true or not, many men still crave
adventure beyond work and home—and often don't know
what to do to fill this need.

My study showed that social activity peaks twice in a marriage. The first peak is in the early years before children. The
second peak comes at the twenty-years-married point. How
important to negate this trend and enjoy an exciting life during the child-raising years, too! Granted, it's not as easy, but
it is essential to the well-being of the marriage.

Traditionally it has been the work of the wife to create
social activities for the family, but, of course, there's no biological reason for this. (Men do know or should learn that
there is more to social life than watching TV and going to
football games.) However, if a couple are going to keep the
joys of married life alive and well, it takes the cooperation of
both mates to create and carry out opportunities for fun and
happy times.

GOOD FRIENDS

One essential element is the building of friendships, with
other couples, with siblings, with singles, and with groups.
My survey overwhelmingly showed that having social times

with others resulted in a happier married life. A little time away lets a couple return to the home circle feeling refreshed.

But good friends also fill other needs. Almost one-third of my survey folks said that they had appreciated the support of friends during a crisis, and that having someone with whom to talk over problems was very helpful. Just realizing that others faced some of the same challenges was very comforting.

Researchers say that the ideal number of close friends is between five and eight. However, having too many friends can be harmful to the marriage relationship when people become over-involved with friends, and frequently talk over problems that are best discussed within the marriage. Although friends can be therapeutic, the spouse should be the chief confidant.

Finding good friends really isn't difficult. Sources include the workplace, clubs, church, civic activities, hobby groups, and neighbors. However, taking the time to cultivate an acquaintance into a friendship does require some effort on your part. It requires your planning time together so that you get to know one another on a comfortable basis. Just as flowers without water fade and wilt, friendships without regular nurturing fade and wilt, too.

THESE DAYS, IS FUN "POLITICALLY CORRECT"?

You know what they say about all work and no play? You make the rules and set the standards for your marriage. Good times are one ingredient of a partnership, perhaps the spice in the recipe for a loving relationship. Don't live a bland, flavorless life waiting for some future opportunity for pleasure. Enjoy it right now.

Here's a potpourri of pleasant suggestions for bringing more joy into married life. Some pertain to good times with friends, some to fun activities to do as a couple, and some to creating happy times right at home.

128 **BE A JOINER**   While you don't want to stretch yourself too thin, belonging to a social group can be one easy way to have fun. This could be a newcomers' group, your church couples' club, or a miniature train society, or other hobby group that interests you. Here you'll meet many couples who are having life experiences similar to yours. But you'll also find people who are quite different, and that can be eye-opening, too.

129 **BE A GOOD SPORT**   It may be silly, but many men are most comfortable at sporting events. Don't let sports put a wall of separation between you and your spouse. Women need to join in and find the fun in these activities. If your husband is a hockey fan, go along and learn what the attraction is beyond the fights. Choose a baseball, football, or basketball team to root for, and attend some games. Invite another couple over to watch a game on TV, talk casually, and eat hot dogs together. In addition to spectator sports, find one you actually enjoy doing together—bowling, tennis, even miniature golf.

130 **EXCURSION DAY**   One couple set aside a day each month for a day-long trip. They started this when the kids were young, sometimes including the children, sometimes leaving them with the grandparents. With the aid of articles from local magazines and newspapers, they compiled a list and a backup file of clippings about interesting places to go. They added to the list regularly, and chose one each month. Parks, shops, museums, gardens, tourist attractions, theaters, restaurants, and interesting back roads provided plenty of choices. They've been enjoying these excursion days for over thirty years and their list of possibilities hasn't dwindled.

A Night Out   It isn't a set-in-cement rule that couples can only go out together. Sometimes a wife enjoys the company of other women and a husband wants a night out with the guys. Gradually society is also accepting the idea of people having platonic friends of the opposite sex, but this is difficult for some people to understand, and can create jealousies. On an occasional basis, a night of bowling, a movie, or a bridge game can be a real refresher. But, it shouldn't take the all-important place of social activities with each other.

131

Tell It Again   Funny happenings are part of the happy fabric of marriage, so learn to laugh together. And repeating these experiences to others just adds to the fun. Some stories get funnier with the retelling (and probably further from the truth). Amusing sayings, babytalk, even mistakes can be repeated to make a light moment. Be careful, though, not to relay an embarrassing experience for your spouse, or tell a story that would result in hurt feelings. While having fun is great, reliving it can be great, too.

132

Cheaper by the Group   When you hold in your hand the actual tickets for an event, you're much more apt to attend. That's why buying tickets to a series of concerts, pops, plays, musicals, or ballgames is a good idea. Such tickets are cheaper than buying them individually, and you'll be less inclined to make up excuses to stay home when you've already paid for them. Should it happen that you can't attend, you probably haven't lost much money, and you can sure win friends by handing the tickets on to someone else.

133

134 **BEDTIME STORIES** Far too many people fail to find time to read books. One wise couple keep an interesting book on the nightstand. Before bed, they take turns reading a chapter to the other. The story becomes a shared experience, another tie in the marriage.

135 **SURPRISE ME** Don't be that kind of husband or wife who just can't think of what to buy for a gift occasion and says, "Here's some cash, go buy something you'd like." While this is better than forgetting the birthday or other event, it doesn't show much creativity. Since you live together, you really do know the person well enough to make a purchase. Buy it where it can be exchanged if necessary, but *do* buy something. This shows you cared enough to take the time and thought to purchase the surprise, and who knows, it might be the perfect choice!

136 **OUR SONG** One couple purchased a cassette of dance music from the years when they were dating. Once every month or so they play it and relive the fun of their younger days when those songs expressed their new-found love. Now they have a toddler who dances right along with them, creating a happy time for all.

137 **ONCE A MONTH** One busy family enjoys entertaining, but only when the house is tidy and their young children are ready for bed. Rather than serve a big dinner and also try to cope with the kids' noise, spilled food, baths, and so forth, they find it easier to get the youngsters to bed and then have friends over for snacks and dessert. So, they plan a monthly get-together with friends and neighbors (the

weekend after the house is cleaned), and they enjoy cha-
rades, trivia and mystery games, and good adult conversation.

138 **SNACK BASKET**   One caring husband
who knows his wife is trying to lose
weight makes TV viewing more enjoyable
by creating a special snack basket for her. Each night it holds
something different: popcorn, pretzels, carrot sticks, low-fat
granola bars, fruit kebabs, plus a low-calorie drink. He says it
keeps her from the temptations in the kitchen and he finds it
fun to come up with something different each day of the
week.

139 **STICKY NOTES**   So often when reading a book, magazine, or newspaper,
one spouse finds something that's likely
to be of special interest to the other. Keep a little tablet of
those sticky notes and affix one to the margin opposite the
article. This results in later conversation about the subject
matter. Couples who talk about issues together are more in
tune with one another.

140 **GRATEFUL GRACE**   One couple didn't
ever say grace until they began attending
church socials, which they really enjoyed.
Hearing grace said there, they decided to have grace at their
own dinnertimes, expressing appreciation for all family members and the good received. And it's their tradition to always
include a special blessing on their beloved spouse.

141 **EXERCISE FUN**   When two work out
together, it can be much more fun than a
lonely solo routine. Choose a time each
day to bend and stretch, do sit-ups, or anything else on your

keep-fit list. You can give words of encouragement or assistance. Get a gym membership together. Take up walking, jogging, in-line skating, tennis, line dancing—all great exercise.

 **142** **A REMEMBRANCE TREE** For a birthday or other special occasion, a spouse sometimes sends flowers, which are lovely for only a few days. Consider a more lasting tribute (and one that can cost less)—a tree. You can get a small one that will be happy indoors or potted on the patio, or one for your garden that will grow big and strong through the years. Plant your yard with "remembrance trees" honoring special occasions. And, it's a touching note to carefully carve a heart with your and your mate's initials in the trunk of an established tree.

143 **SATURDAY MORNING ANGEL** Spouses can take turns being a Saturday morning angel. The angel gets up first. The angel feeds breakfast to the youngsters and encourages them to play quietly or look at a quality video. Then, the angel prepares a special breakfast, puts the newspaper and a flower on the tray, and tiptoes into the bedroom to give a wake-up kiss. The perfect start for a Saturday!

144 **MIRROR MESSAGES** If you want to cheer a spouse and start some fun, write a message on the bathroom mirror. Use shaving cream, a light lipstick, or an easy-to-remove crayon. Ask a question, give a compliment, draw a happy face. See if you get an answer in return.

145 **CONTINUOUS FUN** Competition can be exhilarating! On a hall table, kitchen counter, or other level surface, set up a puzzle or a game board of checkers or chess. See who can finish a difficult section of the puzzle. Have a marker, such as a button or coin, to show what piece you've added or what move you've made in the game. While you may not ever face your opponent, you'll enjoy these thoughtful pauses in a busy day.

146 **BICYCLES BUILT FOR TWO**   Borrow the kids' bikes or buy cheap ones at a garage sale and pedal your way around the neighborhood. Look for a bicycle built for two—a good idea coming back in style. After dinner, go out for a fifteen minute spin. When you return, you'll be surprised how invigorated you are, ready for the evening ahead. And you'll feel good about the exercise and, of course, the companionship.

147 **A SPECIAL DECK OF CARDS**   Turn an old deck of cards into a set of gift coupons for your spouse. On paper, write out each gift offered, cut the papers to fit, and then glue them to the cards. The gift coupons can include: a car wash, massage, hair-brushing, ice cream sundae, moonlight walk, straightening up a workbench or closet, cleaning eye glasses, polishing shoes, a movie— whatever you think your mate would like. Let your spouse choose one card each day. Always reshuffle them before the next day's selection. You can also create a "his" and "hers" deck.

148 **GUESS WHAT I MADE!**   Clip a few interesting but quick and easy-to-prepare recipes out of the weekly food section. These are given to the spouse who cooks the least (or doesn't cook at all). See that necessary ingredients are in the pantry. Then, ask the so-called non-cook to surprise you by making one of the dishes, gently remarking that everyone knows that if you can read, you can cook. You don't have to be dead tired to call in the novice cook! Sometimes it's just fun to take a nap and see what's ready when you wake up. And remember, the more appreciation you show, the more often you may get treated.

149 **GETTING AWAY FROM IT ALL** Plan a regular vacation—be it simple or fabulous, it will be fun. Enjoy the planning stage by researching possibilities at the library, travel agency, or auto club. You can save money by camping or choosing an "off season" for travel. Don't forget the refreshing merits of a minivacation such as one or two nights at a nearby hotel, guest ranch, or bed-and-breakfast. Make a scrapbook about each vacation and enjoy them in retrospect, too.

150 **ASK YOURSELF** If you look longingly back at the old days and all the fun you used to have, ask yourself this question: "What did we do then that we can still do now?" Look at old photos and scrapbooks and talk about the fun times. You'll find that many of those events are easily transferable to the present. Make a list of the best times you've ever had. Then, try to repeat these, and even improve on them.

•   •   •

Don't let your marriage become a casualty due to boredom. Make memorable times every single day. Schedule an enjoyable event for every weekend. Entertain once a month. Find the satisfaction of working in a service group, helping those less fortunate. Take up a hobby. Get out, enjoy the world, and your marriage will be refreshed. Like Ralph and Barb who longed for the early lighthearted days of their marriage, you too will find out how to bring back those happy days.

Getting it all done

Stacey and Neil always knew what they wanted out of their marriage—a fulfilling home life, satisfying work, opportunities for outreach to the community, and time to be together. The problem was fitting those desires into a twenty-four-hour day. They each had nine-to-five jobs and two active teenage sons who still required care, guidance, and chauffeuring.

Because of her accounting skills, Stacey had been roped into being treasurer of two civic groups, as well as having full charge of the household finances. And because Neil traveled for his business and thus had little time to spend with his sons, he felt alienated from them. The kids weren't much better at managing their own needs, complaining that there wasn't enough time in a day for sports, homework, chores, and social events.

Tension caused frequent quarrels and they all realized that something had to give—but they didn't know what. When asked for suggestions, a *well-meaning friend told them that they obviously needed better time-management skills.*

Neil responded, "I don't need more skills, I need more time."

And Stacey snapped, "All I can do is the stuff that's right in front of me. I have no time to learn time management. Just give me an extra hour each day."

That extra hour each day is what many marriages need. And happily, there are ways to get it. *Getting organized and using time wisely are essentials for a strong and lasting marriage.* By systematizing the routine events of life, we have more time for the adventures of life, the important and enjoyable things that truly make a difference.

Don't be fooled into thinking that simple organization and time-management skills are only a part of the workplace and have nothing to do with marriage. They truly do! Many marriages go on the skids because mates have no concept of how to control time, work effectively at home or office, or spend adequate time enjoying each other and the family. Don't let this disorganization become a Master Destroyer in your marriage!

When the Fabulous 400 couples were asked what they'd like more time for, the majority said: "to spend with my mate," "to be with the kids," "to exercise," or "to read." When they listed marriage problems (and they said they'd already worked out most of them), the one that often lingered was how to manage time effectively and how to divide the work in the home. *So there is a strong connection between the judicious use of time and a solid marriage.*

DIVIDING THE WORK FAIRLY

When both spouses work away from home, *both* spouses should perform the work necessary to make the home run effectively. Sounds good, but it doesn't often happen! Unfortunately, most women are still doing the bigger share of the homemaking chores. One wife said, "There he is—reading the evening paper, looking at TV with the kids, taking a little nap. And here I am—cleaning up the kitchen, folding the laundry, walking the dog, writing his mom, helping with the homework, on and on all evening."

In my survey, I found that certain home tasks are usually relegated to the husband or wife. Even today, an overwhelming majority of the women do all the household cleaning, cooking, laundry, and child care. The men take care of the finances, home repairs, and car care. Garden tasks are often divided with wives planting and reaping, men doing the manly mowing, pruning, digging, and raking. But unless there are physical or mental limitations, there is no biological reason for this division of work. Either is capable of any of these tasks.

It's time to throw away such outmoded traditions and make a new policy of equality. One kind husband says, "I don't sit down until my wife does." Bless him! Unfortunately he's more of an exception than current magazine and newspaper articles would have us believe.

Many husbands in my study regretted the unfair division of work, and many wives silently seethed over it. (In answer to the question "Is the division of work fair?" men usually said yes and a majority of women said no.) The men remembered that their mothers, who did not have jobs outside the home, did most of the household tasks. Thus, when women began having careers outside the home, the men allowed the old ways to continue, not realizing that the majority of women were essentially holding down two jobs. This situation added frustration and tension to the marriage.

But there is another reason for the unfair division of work. For some emotional reason, perhaps because they don't want to seem incompetent, women are senselessly hesitant about asking for help. They'll gratefully accept it if offered, but they won't say, "Could you please give me a hand with the vacuuming?"; "I'm tired, could you get dinner on the table?"; or "How 'bout helping Junior with his homework?" It's time women quit covering up the anger and disappointment caused by the disparity of work and spoke out, asking for the help they rightfully deserve. At the same time, men should do more than lend a helping hand; they should volunteer to do a fair share.

CREATING A LEVEL PLAYING FIELD

Getting out of the rut of routine is essential to correcting this inequity and to learning ways of best managing time. Both husband and wife have to be willing—even eager—to try different ways. Sometimes a new system takes additional work at the start before it can become a timesaver, so both spouses have to be patient. And, of course, the cooperation of both the spouses (and children) is needed to give any new idea a fair trial. (You may have to uncover and correct that hidden attitude of wanting a new system to fail.)

Saving time through more intelligent division of work and responsibility immeasurably improves a marriage and can provide that "extra hour" so needed in a busy day. Timesaving ideas fall in several categories: saving time by being better organized, saving time in doing chores around the house, saving time at work, saving time in volunteer activities. Gaining minutes and hours in these areas and being in charge of one's time creates a feeling of self-control, calmness, and peace. Thus one is not always functioning at the whims of others or by the constraints of the clock.

Here are several dozen tested-and-approved suggestions that can give you that extra hour each day, an hour that you can use to build memorable moments in family and married life.

GETTING IT ALL TOGETHER

Running a home is a big business, yet many spouses ignore the myriad good business principles that could make it run more effectively. To appreciate this, total up the *yearly* cost of your home mortgage or rent, insurance, food, clothing, entertainment, children's education, health care, transportation, and other major expenses. Then multiply that number by 50 to give you a rough idea of the importance of careful home management through the years of your marriage. Perhaps you'll see the importance of getting your act together!

151 **A HOME IS A BUSINESS** Create a home office as the center for family organization. Have a desk with phone, adding machine, typewriter or computer, bulletin board, supply drawer, and file drawer. Create a file for each family member, each club or activity in which you participate, warranties, birth and marriage certificates, pets, holiday ideas and gift-giving, entertaining, recipes, budget, excursions, catalog orders placed, correspondence, medical records, tax records, memberships, subscriptions, credit cards, home improvement ideas, photographs, investments, bank accounts, and whatever else you want to keep—and later find. Now go to this desk once each day!

152 **INDEPENDENT MORNINGS** Who likes being awakened? No one! See that all family members have simple alarm clocks and know how to use them. Let them know that the morning activities (washing, dressing, tidying room, doing chores, having breakfast, then brushing teeth) are their own responsibilities. Rotate the lunch-making duties among those who require lunch. Have a "Going Shelf" near the exit door to place those things that are to go out that day (lunches, books, cleaning, Scout cookies, attaché case, exercise clothes, etc.)

Charge kids (about one to three dollars) for morning chauffeuring if they miss their carpool or bus. If kids don't get up on time, they must be sleepy, so set their bed times earlier until they learn to get up and do what's necessary for a calm and happy morning. A good send-off is important to husbands and wives as well as other family members since the hours ahead will be the longest time of separation from one another.

153 **BULLETIN BOARD LISTS** Don't rely on trying to remember all the important—or trifling—details of life. Teach family members to write things down on the bulletin board lists: weekly grocery list (it's a waste of time to go more often), repair list (for the Saturday morning handy person), loaned list (otherwise you'll never know where your possessions are), telephone list (emergency numbers and close friends). For you and your spouse, create a stuff-that-we-hope-to-do list that you can add to or cross off when achieved. And if you have children, there should be a list of approved TV shows, the family rules and what happens when they're broken, and a fairly divided list of tasks to be done daily and weekly.

154 **THE FAMILY CALENDAR** Essential to knowing who is where, and when there will be free time, is a calendar showing meetings, appointments, classes, recitals, club meeting dates, important errands, sports, and social events. Refer to it daily and if there is too much going on, rearrange (or cancel) some events so there is relaxing time at home. Families who are always on the go don't have sufficient time to enjoy one another's company—an essential for any lasting relationship.

155 ### Paper Work

Buy an accordion bring-up or tickler file numbered for the thirty-one days of the month. Open the mail daily and immediately throw away the envelopes and any unwanted junk mail. Put bills in this file (under the fifteenth and thirtieth for paying on time so you'll avoid late charges.) Under the proper date, file tickets, invitations, things you want to consider later in the month, items to take along when going out such as your meeting report or the driving instructions to an event, short reminder messages, letters to answer, birthday cards to be mailed (write these the first of the month and then put them under the mailing date), and anything else with a time deadline. Take charge of paper work and don't let it bury you. This kind of organization will eliminate forgetfulness that can upset you, causing stress in the marriage.

POWER HOME MAINTENANCE

While cleaning and maintenance are important, these activities should not be the highlights of the weekend. Get the jobs done and then get on to more important things. It's a lot easier if home tasks are done by pairs or as a group—this gives opportunities for light conversation as well as learning how to both give and take suggestions—skills we can all use.

156 ### Room-a-Day

Few people nowadays have time for the old-fashioned once-a-week "cleaning day," so do a few chores each day. Clean the easier/smaller rooms on your busier days. Should you be having friends over, clean the living room and family room the day before. Make your cleaning fun by turning on music, a book on tape, a good TV show, or by sharing the work with your spouse or kids. Have your larger supplies organized in a caddie (that plastic tray with a handle) and wear a carpenter's apron for small supplies—this keeps everything handy at your fingertips. A feather duster makes quick work of areas like book shelves and spice racks.

Of course, not everything needs cleaning each week. Make a schedule for once-a-month, every-other-month, or quarterly tasks such as dusting picture frames, light bulbs and lamps, washing windows, cleaning the refrigerator, polishing door hardware, polishing wood floors, putting up screens, and so forth. An orderly house can be a source of contentment for both spouses.

157 BEST FRIENDS

Two wives whose husbands play golf together clean their houses together while the guys are gone. First they do one house, have a snack, then the other. The house owner does the kitchen and baths, and the other wife dusts and vacuums. They've done this for years and have a wonderful time talking and working together. And when the golfers return, the women are ready to be taken out to dinner!

158 IF YOU HAVE KIDS

With the help of your children, tackle one room at a time. By working together, an average room can be cleaned in ten to fifteen minutes. (To put everyone in the spirit, put a cassette of Sousa marches in a tape player and carry it from room to room as you work.) One helper takes everything off surfaces, another dusts, and the first one puts stuff back. Another delivers out-of-place items to other rooms and does the bend-over work of dusting baseboards or hand-vacuuming the edges of the room or under beds and furniture. The parent in charge does the main vacuuming until a child is old enough to do it—you'll find that young kids like vacuuming!

If kids prefer to do the cleaning on their own, use this method: write on 3″ x 5″ cards the needed tasks: dusting, vacuuming, cleaning bathrooms, floor washing/polishing. On the first of the month each family member draws a card with a once-a-week duty for that month. You are doing your children a favor by showing them what it takes to maintain a home. And you'll find family members more appreciative of home if they take part in caring for it.

159 **TIME SAVERS** Looking for misplaced items is a big waste of time that can cause friction between husbands and wives. One spouse shouldn't be constantly asked to locate missing items or accused of misplacing them! Rather, each family member should be accountable. Every time you walk through the house, make it a habit to pick up something and put it where it belongs. Or, have a box in the family room where out-of-place items will be put until their owner looks for them. Empty it once a month when all the family is present. Teach kids and spouses to put things "where they go" as opposed to "where they fall."

160 **NOT JUST FOR SPRINGTIME** Leaving out busy months such as November and December, assign a month to each area of the house. Spend about fifteen minutes each week of that month putting that room/closet/garage in order. And while you're doing it, set aside unused items to donate to charity. If you have children still at home, let them earn extra money by cleaning drawers, shelves, and cupboards for you. Assign a dollar or cents amount to each area and post it on a sticky note on the drawer or door. Each child can sign up for the areas he/she wishes to clean in one week's time. Give simple instructions and insist they be followed. Then sit back and let others do the work for you! The time saved will give you another opportunity to enjoy an activity with your spouse or children.

161 **LOVING THE LAUNDRY** Family strife arises when clothes are not clean and ready to be worn, so get a handle on this easy task. Next to the washer and dryer, have bins labeled for each kind of load: wash and wear, whites, jeans/dark pants and socks, delicate/hand wash, and items to be cleaned. Make family members responsible for putting their dirty clothes in the proper bins. (Items put in incorrect bins don't get washed that week.) Anytime a bin is full, run that load. Put clean clothes on a nearby counter or shelf labeled with family member names. It's each person's job to take away clean laundry.

Family members should pile their dirty sheets on the laundry floor until washed. When washed, they are placed on the proper bed for bed making. Sometimes this chore is more quickly done in pairs.

Tack on the wall an envelope for special care tags so you can check them easily. When buying clothes, one mother permits kids to buy clothes that require ironing only if that child promises to do the ironing. If you must iron, do it in front of the TV or invite a friend over to chat. And remember, neither changing sheets nor doing the ironing is a gender-related task.

162 **THIRTY-MINUTE WONDERS** Just thirty minutes spent once each week —perhaps on Saturday morning—should keep you on top of repairs. Work as a husband/wife team (this preserves togetherness) or as a parent/child team (this is educational fun). Work from that list posted on the bulletin board. If broken toys are to be repaired, be sure the toy owner takes part. Keeping up-to-date on repairs helps to eliminate marital nagging.

163 **THE NOT-SO-GREAT OUTDOORS** If you don't need a garden, don't have one. Plant your grounds with easy-care shrubs and ground covers. However, if you like grass and flower beds, make upkeep a joint effort. With kids, let each specialize in a flower bed of easy-to-grow zinnias or snapdragons, or a plot of squash or tomatoes.

Set up a watering schedule and make this a different person's chore each month. Every-other-week upkeep is necessary, but punctuate the work with games or races, and a lemonade and granola bar snack. Some workers enjoy listening to the radio. Save time by pulling weeds when they're small or using an emergent herbicide to catch them early.

To weed a lawn rapidly, spread string to make large squares. Then, assign each family member to a square. Offer a prize to the one who can pull the most weeds (but insist on the roots, too).

If you truly like outdoor living, make your yard another room of the house by arranging comfortable seating on patio or deck areas, making a place for outdoor cooking, and creating areas for croquet or badminton, a swing or tree house. In pleasant weather, you'll have many memorable family events in your outdoor room. Make it a habit to sit outside a moment at the end of the day.

GET ME TO THE JOB ON TIME!

On the job, you need good time management to make the most of those eight hours; however, nothing ruins a day more than a late start from home. (The same goes for arriving late at social events.) Tardiness, with its associated stress, can creep into the entire day and that late person is then upsetting not only to a spouse and children but also to coworkers and friends.

While everyone is late occasionally, chronically late persons say many unbecoming things about themselves:

- They're not intelligent enough to figure out how long it takes to get from bed to work.
- They're too cheap to call to say they're going to be late.
- They're so selfish about their own time that they don't mind making others wait for them.
- They're inconsiderate and don't care about those worrying over their whereabouts (or wasting a good meal).
- They're dull people and use lateness as a way of getting attention.

Here are ideas for getting you places on time and helping you to work effectively once you are there. And you may ask what this has to do with a good marriage? An efficient worker usually has a more successful job record and thus greater income, leading to a more satisfying home life—and that results in a happier marriage.

While most of these ideas are for desk work at home or on the job, many of the concepts are useful for those lucky folks not tied down to the desk chair from nine to five.

164 **STARTING THE DAY POSITIVELY** The mood of the day is set in the first thirty minutes. Figure out how long your morning preparations take and get up at the proper time, adding ten extra minutes for last-minute emergencies. Brush your teeth immediately (it jogs your brain into action and your loved one will appreciate it), shower, take time for prayer or meditation, read a peppy motto you've put on your mirror, listen to the news as you dress, then, most important, allow time for a nutritious breakfast and *pleasant* conversation with the family, and finally make a calm, on-time departure.

Mirror mottos could be: "I'm a wonderful and talented person." "Diamonds are just little chunks of coal that stuck to their jobs." "Organized people have time to make whoopie!"

165 CURES FOR LATENESS Your spouse, friends, and business associates can be angry with you if you're always late, so get on the ball. First, time yourself at getting ready to leave home (see number 164). Also, write down the time it takes you to get to the usual places you go. Then, start your dressing and leaving home in time to be five minutes early. It's childish, but keep your watch and home clocks set five minutes ahead. Mark your calendar ten minutes earlier for events—for example, show a 9:30 A.M. meeting as 9:20. Should you arrive early, use the time to make pleasant conversation.

In your datebook or calendar, put a red check mark for on-time successes, and a blue check mark for lateness. Reward yourself when the reds outnumber the blues. Lateness isn't a cute habit that people will accept and overlook; it can harm business success as well as marriage and social relationships, so work hard to overcome it.

166 THE PAPER TRAP At the office or at home, always start on today's work, not the leftovers of the previous day. Keep today's work in a red folder. When you have a handle on it, look at leftover work (kept in a blue folder) and you may find some of it is no longer necessary. Don't postpone decisions unless absolutely necessary. Look at the mail only once, putting each item in the today file, to do later file, reading file, filing file, or wastebasket.

Make good use of file cabinets by maintaining a simple filing system. Ask yourself: "If I wanted this information later, where would I look for it?" Throw away more than you file.

Use a highlighter to mark important parts of articles so that you don't have to reread the entire piece to find the information you need. Stay up to date on your computer literacy. Create a good work environment with necessary supplies and a comfortable chair.

MANAGING DESK TIME   Start the **167** day by doing something quick and easy. Then, feeling successful, tackle the most difficult job on your list. Save phone calls for a midmorning break; this leaves most of the day for a return call. For greatest efficiency, most people should do numbers work early in the day, reading when it is most quiet, and writing work when hungry. (There is no logical reason for this—most folks just write better on an empty stomach!) Avoid time-wasting gossip at copy machines and snack machines, saving socializing for lunchtime. When someone comes to see you, pick up a pad and pencil to show that you are businesslike and plan to write down their good ideas. This will help keep their conversation on the point at hand.

ACCOMPLISHING GOALS   Make both **168** short- and long-term business and family goals. Break large projects into smaller ones. On your calendar, block out segments of time to be sure you finish a project on schedule. Get reports completed forty-eight hours in advance so you can go over your work before presentation. Reward yourself for finishing a project (do something enjoyable, get a soft drink, phone your spouse).

Play a game with yourself by listing the day's work and estimating the time for each job. See if you can keep on schedule and be alert to where you take more time than the project is worth. Pick out a stimulating task for the three-in-the-afternoon mental slump. Thirty minutes before the end of the workday, tidy your work area, put leftover work in the blue folder, tomorrow's priority work in the red folder, and set up your first morning task. This will allow the shift between office and home to be stress-free and your spouse will see you at peace with yourself and the world.

169 **BETTER MEETINGS** Whether the meeting is at work or for a community activity, you will be happier if you come on time, prepared, and with a good attitude. Smile at the person speaking. Make notes on what you're to do. Look alive. Follow the agenda and stick to the topic.

Consider if now is the time for a decision (or more information is needed) and if this is the group to make the decision (or the project belongs to some other group). Don't carry on a whispered conversation and don't interrupt the speaker. Ask for a midpoint break if a meeting will last more than ninety minutes.

Be solution oriented, talking more about solving the problem than the problem itself. Don't be negative; be willing to try new ideas. Be sure decisions are possible, positive, practical, painless (not hurting others), and democratic.

A TIME FOR ACTIVITIES

Be selective when choosing community activities and don't let them preempt all-important time for your mate and children. There should be a balance between home and community, with greater weight given to family.

170 **JUST SAY NO** When spouses overextend themselves on civic/church/club activities, marriages may flounder due to neglect. Ask yourself, "If I don't do this, will it not get done? And if it doesn't get done, will the world collapse?" Certainly say yes to activities that are important to your life, but gauge how much you can do effectively without penalizing your home life. Sometimes repeating the same activity (such as a chairmanship) year after year keeps others from trying their wings. Don't get typecast in a certain office. You'll enjoy activities more if you try different ones—some on your own, some with your spouse.

171 **MEMORY BUILDING** Good marriages are built on good memories. See that your schedule has ample time for regularly planned social activities with each other, children, family, and friends. Organize a progressive supper, a Valentine potluck, an Academy Award party, a neighborhood barbecue, a street party, a cards and games night, or birthday and holiday celebrations. Look at your calendar regularly and see that these occur often. That way, years from now, you can look back on the married years with great satisfaction.

172 **A BEST-EVER ACTIVITY** If you have little time for community interaction, your church is the best single activity. Why? Because it provides for your well-being in so many different ways. It gives you spiritual awareness and comfort, it provides education and enlightenment for all your family, it strengthens you in difficult times, it lets you reach out to the community, and it connects you with people who can be part of your wider circle of friends.

Research shows that there is less divorce between couples who participate in church activities. Fabulous 400 couples call church activities "what draws us closer together," "the cement of our relationship," "the right start for the entire week," "a refuge in hard times," "a common bond with our children," and "a beacon light that guides our lives."

MORE READING, LESS TELEVISION

173 Many wives complain that their husbands are "couch potatoes," settling into the TV-viewing chair immediately after supper and never moving until bedtime. One of my Fabulous 400 couples says that they enjoy evenings of no TV at all, instead reading separately or often aloud from a mutually interesting book.

Newspapers and catalogs can be read during TV time, but serious reading requires a background of good music or just plain quiet. Couples find that reading articles on the same or similar subjects is intellectually stimulating and they can have a good discussion of the issues with each other.

Save TV-viewing as a treat and while sitting in front of it, make menus, clip coupons, do puzzles, mend, make small repairs, and talk to each other during the commercials. Instead of the repetitive and depressing late news, try a moonlight walk together before bed.

TOGETHERNESS TIME

174 The best use of your free time is to interact with your spouse and family. This caring attitude can be expressed in sharing a variety of activities together. One couple exercise together, sometimes with their teenage sons. Another couple enjoy a small gauge railroad; they enjoy building miniature towns and mountains as well as just playing with the trains. Saturdays are spent together visiting hobby and craft shops and shows. Another couple find that doing work projects together is a satisfying way of "staying in touch." Don't just live under the same roof. A home is a special haven for just the two of you. *Invent and invest in meaningful togetherness each day.*

AN EXTRA HOUR

175 To gain an hour or more each day, try some of these tested ideas from the Fabulous 400.

- Look at one less TV show—gain thirty minutes daily.
- Use a timer when on the phone and make shorter calls—gain two minutes daily.
- Combine errands and do several on one trip—gain thirty minutes weekly.
- Try to learn from past mistakes and save time by not repeating them—gain immeasurable time!
- Be firm about youngsters' bedtimes and put them to bed early enough so you two have time together—gain thirty minutes to spend with each other. (It's a fact that most kids nowadays don't go to bed at a reasonable hour and thus awake tired and unready to be attentive in school.)
- Let mates and kids help around the house—gain sixty or more minutes daily.
- Be organized at work; an uncluttered desk will let you work faster—gain ten minutes daily.
- Be organized in home activities such as cooking in quantity— gain ten minutes daily.
- Avoid repeat experiences or boring activities (such as serving as club treasurer for five consecutive years)— gain thirty minutes monthly.
- Determine the proper amount of sleep you need and cut back on oversleeping—gain twenty to forty minutes daily. (Do this by setting the alarm five minutes earlier each week. If you don't feel more tired than the week before, take off another five minutes the next week. Most folks will be able to work up to twenty to forty minutes less sleep nightly over the course of several months.)

Now use all this saved time for something worthwhile together!

•   •   •

We have two gifts we can give our spouses: one is our time, the other is our ability. Ability is unlimited and we can love, help, listen, guide, teach, entertain, encourage. But time seems limited so we need to make the very best use of each minute we have. The wasted minute is never given back.

Think about the time you *do* have, not the time you *don't* have. That's what Stacey and Neil's disorganized family did— they're still working on it, but they're making some progress.

What's the use of saving time if you don't have someone you love to spend it with? Even if you have only five spare minutes, use them well. This proper use of time can make you a better person, a better parent and friend, and best of all, a better spouse.

$Dollars and ¢Sense

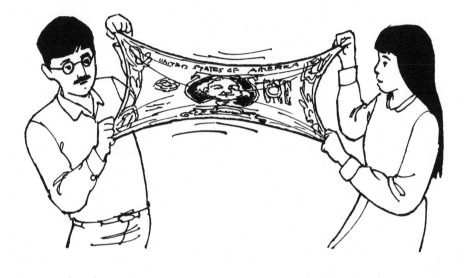

Josh stared grimly at the credit card bills, unable to believe the interest charges that had crept higher and higher each month. He pawed through the litter of checks and charge receipts on the dining room table, wondering if they could ever get ahead. Then he shook his head and buried it in his hands. When Liz brought in cold milk and chocolate cookies—his favorites—he realized that not even this could cheer him.

"We're really in the hole now," he muttered. Liz sighed in frustration. "I don't know where the money goes, so it's probably my fault," He slowly nodded in agreement.

She sat down next to him and took his hand, realizing that money problems were tearing their marriage apart. In tears she said, "I wish we could work this out together."

Working out family finances together is a great idea—and it usually brings great results. Too often one marriage partner tries to do it all alone, but it's really a joint responsibility. Normally one partner will be in charge of balancing accounts or planning savings or recommending major expenditures, but the overall plan must be designed and supported by both partners.

Money (the spending and the saving) is a major cause of divorce. Money can cause a rift if there's not enough or even when there's too much. This Master Destroyer can cause arguments when it is squandered or when it is hoarded. Money can be an emotional issue because of a fixation on it or the lackadaisical care of it.

In my study, couples said it was the chief cause of disagreements in the first two decades of marriage. But the Fabulous 400 had some ideas to help any marriage get a firm grip on the dollars and sense of living within their income.

Let some of these ideas help you gain control of your money matters:

176 **NONSEXIST**   Money management is no longer the male prerogative with the woman being given an allowance to run the house and the man taking charge of everything else. Invariably one partner earns more money than the other, but this is no basis for giving that partner the right to be the sole decider on how money should be spent. Early in marriage it is vital to make money a joint interest.

Dividing responsibility can make both partners pros, especially if you switch the duties yearly. These money tasks should be divvied up and traded off: balancing the checkbook, making deposits, checking receipts against charges and paying charge accounts, recommending savings and investments, deciding allowances for kids, providing cash to each family member, keeping records for tax time, making sure that any regular income checks have come in, and so forth.

MINE OR OURS?

177 MINE OR OURS? Newly married couples sometimes consider the benefits of maintaining separate accounts versus pooling their income. But long-married couples say that separate accounts can lead to secrecy and hurt feelings. Be upfront about money—what you have and how you use it. Try to make it "our money" rather than "my money." It doesn't matter if one partner works hard to bring home a paycheck and the other works hard at running the house and raising children. Let it be a co-partnership. Mutual trust, respect, and affection is garnered by sharing all the resources available to a relationship, and these resources include time and ability as well as income.

178 FINANCIAL "FILOSOPHY" A wise man has said, "Live with *minimum* outflow, for this is the mark of an intelligent person." Of course, *maximum* outflow can lead to self-destruction. We can all learn something from many of the fabulously rich who have this motto: "Spend interest but never principal." However, that's not possible until one has enough money to have some investments! Should that happy time come, it is good advice. But, in the meantime, be the intelligent person with minimum outflow.

179 A PLACE TO START Until you have a firm grip on your finances, keep a record of every dollar spent. Use a budget book to record checks and deposits as well as cash expenditures. Review it monthly and make an assessment each quarter so that a yearly budget can eventually be made. Each partner should keep a small card on which to list all cash expenditures. As excess pocket money is just a temptation to spend frivolously, carry just enough money to take care of your weekly cash needs.

THE CASH SYSTEM   Some families **180** function well with a cash system, avoiding check-writing and charges—even paying utilities, mortgage, and phone bills with cash. This is often called the "envelope system" and, since you can't just leave envelopes of cash lying around, it requires a safe place to keep the money. For each expenditure (food, transportation, meals out, clothing, entertainment, miscellaneous), the allotted cash is put in a marked envelope. When the envelope is empty, that's the end of spending in that category (unless there is money in the miscellaneous envelope that should only be used by mutual agreement). Each month, money put in the envelopes can be adjusted for special needs.

SELF-DISCIPLINE   Many people exer- **181** cise wisdom in every area but money. If you are not naturally responsible monetarily and have spendthrift tendencies, you may not be able to handle the enticing habit of dashing off checks or whipping out the plastic charge card. Yes, it's SOOOO easy to be attracted by new clothes or new "things," but lack of self-discipline can lead to financial doom. An undisciplined spender is better off dealing with cash, although that doesn't usually provide a good record of spending. But it is better than running wild with checks and charge cards. The best answer is to become self-disciplined when it comes to spending.

THE LIVING BUDGET   Few married **182** couples look forward to the night when the budget for the new year is prepared! Yet, every couple should have a budget—in times of poverty as well as in times of affluence—since it is a good record of how expectations are carried out. Use columnar paper to show each category (food, rent, utilities, clothes, etc.), then follow it with the actual expenditure for the previous year and the proposed expenditure for this year. A budget shouldn't be too rigid or too fluid, however. Although it may seem that certain categories contain too much or too little money for the upcoming months, don't rush to change the budget after only one or two months. Seasonal needs may balance out the monthly totals. If a few categories are really lopsided after a six-month period, it's acceptable to juggle the figures around. Make a file for these yearly budgets and regularly look back for creeping expenditures.

183 **COMPUTER ACCOUNTING**   Financial record-keeping has taken a leap forward with several user-friendly computer programs. The advertising motto for one is "Manage your finances without a fight." If you have a home computer, this will be the most efficient way of governing your funds. But you must remember to use it, feeding into it every expenditure over one dollar. A computer program (just like a handwritten budget plan) can quickly reveal where your spending has gotten out of control. A computer plays no favorites, just telling the facts about overspending, so try hard not to get angry with your computer!

184 **TWO DEMONS**   What two little devils are most apt to tempt us into wrecking the family budget? The most common budget excesses are caused by impulse purchases and eating out. If you're having a hard time making ends meet, cut back on meals away from home or costly prepared meals brought home. The frequent purchase of take-out foods and home-delivered pizza can really add up. Home cooking may take longer, but it costs a whole lot less. (You will also find that it is timesaving to make and freeze a week's sandwiches on Saturday morning as well as to cook and freeze several main courses at a time.) As for the demon of impulse purchases: make a written mutual promise to have a forty-eight-hour waiting period plus a husband/wife consultation before going off the deep end and making any unplanned purchase. You'll often find that the purchase isn't as intriguing after the cooling-off period.

185 **THE GIFT BUDGET**   Couples like to buy gifts for one another, however, these love-offerings can throw a budget out of control unless there is an amount in the budget allotted for gifts. Plan ahead and decide together how much you can afford to spend for birthdays, anniversaries, Valentine's Day, Christmas, and so forth, then stick to the budget. Try to buy these gifts throughout the year at sales or when you see good bargains. It's nice to budget a little extra for a "just because" gift now and then.

186 **BREAKFAST TABLE DECOR**
One young couple keep the check register on the breakfast table since they each write checks on the same account. They look at the balance each morning and then can spend with confidence or wariness during the day.

187 **TAKE THE PLEDGE**   The embarrassment plus the extra time and expense of being overdrawn should be a sufficient cure for that sin. But some foolish dreamers think that certain checks may not be cashed right away and it's OK to write a check when the checkbook balance is on zero. Bad planning! Husbands and wives should make an agreement to *never* write a check on an empty account and risk being charged for insufficient funds. Better yet, they should stop writing checks when the account is at $150.00 or less, just in case one has forgotten to record a check.

188 **THE SECRET CUSHION** Sometimes it can be helpful to fool ourselves. One married couple has long used the "secret cushion" method to keep from being overdrawn. They put an extra $100.00 in the checking account, but did not note the deposit except on the last page of the checkbook. Thus, there's always a small amount there to cover any temporary monetary glitch.

189 **CUT THE CARDS IN HALF** Handy as they are, credit cards are a costly convenience. They lure you into thinking that you'll have enough cash *next* month to cover the purchase, yet so often you don't. It may not be apparent that the item can cost you far more than the original price. First, there can be a yearly fee for the credit card. And second, and most important, if you don't pay the account on time, you're charged interest at the rate of 14 to 20 percent—the nightmare of compounding interest working against you. So close some accounts entirely, cut way back on the number of credit cards you carry, and only purchase what you can pay for the next month.

190 **ONE WONDERFUL CARD** Many couples have found that it pays to have just one credit card, to pay the bill for it *on time*, and to reap benefits from it. This type of card gives you something extra in return for your charges. One card company will replace any charged item that is lost, stolen or broken. Another card rewards you with free gasoline. Another will provide

expensive gift wrapping free of charge and also give you gift certificates for spending a certain amount. But probably the best is
the one that gives you airline miles for each dollar spent. One
Fabulous 400 couple gets a free trip each year because they pay
for almost all their purchases via this single card.

191 **FIRST HOUSE FUND**   When saving
for something as important as a home,
probably the largest investment you'll
ever make, it helps to have a separate fund. That way, you
can't easily dip into it. Name the account for yourselves: The
Jones Family Home Fund. No matter how little, add to it regularly, possibly using a payroll deduction sent directly to the
account. Having a home of your own will add immeasurable
pleasure to your marriage. And, it will let you save money in
the long run since you won't be throwing it away on rent. Let
the first house be a fixer-upper and then, as equity builds,
trade up.

192 **KEEP A ROOF OVER YOUR HEAD**
Save worry, time, and a postage stamp by
having your home mortgage paid directly
to the loan company out of your earnings (an automatic payroll deduction). Then, there will be no temptation to put it off
or spend the money elsewhere. But, you do have to remember to enter the transaction in your checkbook. In some
areas, other recurring bills such as utilities can also be paid
automatically for you.

193 **LOOKING AHEAD**   The hardest task in
money management is setting aside savings. Today, you can have this done automatically, and many who use this method say that since they
don't *see* the money, they don't miss it. Consider savings sys-
tems such as IRAs, 401K plans, and Keough accounts. Often

an employer will make a regular contribution so you get ahead faster. And, many of these plans have definite tax advantages, saving you even more.

194 **LOOKING FURTHER AHEAD**   If you think that Social Security is either social or secure, think again! Saving for a comfortable retirement should start early in marriage. This may not be easy to do when there are the responsibilities of a growing family, but actuaries recommend putting aside 5 percent of salary in the early years, and working up to 15 percent by age forty. Investigate just how your company retirement plan invests money and safeguards it for you. And be sure that company plans provide for your funds being transferred if you change jobs.

195 **FAD-FREE**   The health gurus tell us to eat fat-free. But we should also cut the fat out of expenditures by living fad-free. Responding to fads—buying something the moment it comes on the market (at its highest price)—makes money rapidly fly away. Make sure that major as well as minor purchases are a good value. Buy fewer things, but buy good things that will last. Faddish bargains and voguish buys may seem wise at the moment, but in the end you'll probably spend more replacing out-of-date styles and poorly made merchandise.

196 **WONDERFUL WINDFALLS**   Uncle Joe leaves you a thousand dollars, Uncle Sam gives you a tax refund, the boss gives you a bonus, the long-awaited raise comes through. Bingo! You have some extra money! Let it make a difference in your life—don't just fritter it away. Save some. Spend some. Reward yourself. Decide together to do something very special with the money. Remember, you got along without it, so do something memorable with it.

197 **TEEN BUDGETS**   What kids spend on clothes and entertainment can exasperate parents, cause arguments, and leave a big hole in the folks' finances. To teach money management, begin when children enter kindergarten by giving them an allowance to cover little extras, entertainment, savings, and family gifts. Using money given them at birthdays or Christmas, help them open a savings account. Let them spend half and save half of such gifts.

Then, when kids become preteens, devise a budget for clothes and entertainment. Teach them that the allotted money will provide, for example, two good-looking shirts, or one faddish name-brand shirt. Let them manage these funds and learn from their mistakes, hopefully saving them from grief or embarrassment later in life when their purchases involve large sums of money.

198 **THE BIG C**   College is the big C (for Cost) for many families. The ever-rising cost of a college education terrorizes many parents and unbalances many marriages. Education costs are certainly one cause of the falling birthrate! How can a family with growing children amass the funds for college? A few answers: kid's part-time jobs, a college savings account, searching out scholarships (many awards go begging and are never given), attending a local junior college before going away to school, or hoping that the grandparents will help finance the education. As one dad put it, "It really bit me big." To avoid that big bite, start an education fund *when each child is born*. A small amount set aside monthly can really compound over the eighteen years. Let the kids in on the details of the account so that they too can contribute to their future.

199 **WALLET WIZARDRY**   It's so embarrassing to find one's wallet empty! So you'll never be totally and completely out of funds, do what one couple did over thirty years ago after going out to dinner and finding that neither had any cash with them. From then on, each put a twenty-dollar bill in an unused wallet compartment. As this couple's four kids went off to college, the dad gave each a twenty-dollar bill to keep out of sight, with the understanding that he would ask to see it at each vacation time. (Yes, he'd put a hidden mark on it!) This was called "comfort cash" for real emergency needs. Three of their four children graduated with the same twenty-dollar bill hidden away! What the fourth child did with his mad money is another long story.

200 **THE LOCKING GAS CAP**

A new invention can provide safety and peace of mind for less than twenty dollars. It is the locking gas cap, now available for most every model car. This sturdy cap, which replaces the regular cap, has a combination (which you choose) that foils anyone trying to open your tank and syphon your gas. However, when you remove the gas cap, there is a secret compartment inside the cover that can hold a rolled-up bill and a car door key. That way you'll always have twenty dollars or so for an emergency, and a way to get into your car should you misplace your keys. It's much cheaper than having a locksmith break into your car for you.

201 **DISCRETIONARY FUNDS**   One couple felt that having some money that they didn't need to account to the other for gave them a feeling of independence. At first they were always in debt because they abused this luxurious habit. Eventually they agreed on a small "no questions asked" sum, and if they felt the need for larger discretionary funds, they found another way to save it or earn it.

PENNY-PINCHING   A new business **202** has sprung up with clubs and newsletters just for tightwads. Given our current income tax structure, spending ten dollars less is worth nearly twice as much as earning ten dollars more, so pinching pennies can add up! Consider these tightwad ideas: shop for clothes at end-of-season sales, use tie spray to protect expensive ties, buy furniture only at discount, use generic brands of cleaning supplies and cosmetics, install ceiling fans to cut air-conditioning bills, eat out at lunch where you get the same food as at dinner but at a lower price, finance your car through a home equity loan rather than a car loan, use ground turkey rather than ground beef, store reusable food in wraps and containers to preserve its quality, and shop when supermarkets aren't crowded so you can more easily assess the best buys. Share penny-pinching ideas with your spouse and with the money saved, spend some on an item you both really want and also put some in the savings account.

BANKRUPTCY—NOT AN OPTION **203** Don't let finances reach the point of your having to throw in the towel. This option is really not an option if you are a responsible person who wouldn't dream of hurting others as well as wrecking your own credit. Bankruptcy doesn't just suddenly appear! It comes on gradually with many warning signs such as a continually unbalanced budget, increasing debts, juggling one payment against another, making foolish investments, gambling, looking for quick fixes, unmerited borrowing, and hoping for undeserved miracles. For most people, ever-increasing credit card balances is the leading indicator. Soon everything financial is beginning to work against you because you didn't pay attention to the warnings.

Bankruptcy ruins your credit rating for at least seven years.

You can't borrow money for a house or car. Your credit report is lousy. You're perceived as someone who can't be trusted. Make a strong pact with your spouse that you will not let these terrible things spoil your marriage. Stop buying anything but necessities, work out a plan with creditors, gain a little each paycheck, and get back on a pay-as-you-go basis.

•   •   •

One wife summed up money problems this way: "They say that the love of money is the root of all evil. I say that ignoring money matters until they get out of control is the real root of all evil. We learned early on that our love for each other was far more important than amassing material things, so we always made sure we had a valid reason for spending. And with that philosophy we found we had that greater love for each other, and at the same time we got some of the material things, too."

Josh and Liz felt much the same way. Now, five years after their big money crunch, they say they have a handle on what they spend and save, and that money is no longer an eroding issue in their otherwise solid marriage.

You said "I do"—so do it

What is it that makes a marriage really click? Why do some marriages last six months or six years and others stay strong for sixty years? How come some couples are victorious over the Master Destroyers of marriage and others fall victim? In the preceding chapters we've discussed those elements that contribute to a lasting marriage. But there is one more: the *determination* to make it work and work well. This must come first, but I've put it last so it will be clearly remembered.

Each of you must be mentally and physically dedicated to keeping your relationship loving, vital, fresh, and lasting. And this doesn't just happen by magic, by wishful thinking, or by a sudden quick-fix solution.

When you said those simple words "I do," your vow was based on the knowledge you then had at hand. But now, you have more knowledge about your mate and marriage. You may like some of what you've learned; you may hate some of it. So what are you going to do?

Your response should not be one of turning your back on what bothers you and ultimately ending the relationship. For a lasting marriage, you have two better choices: (1) accept the problem and determine to live with it without letting it eat you, or (2) find ways to work together to alleviate the problem.

The experiences of our Fabulous 400 show that there is wisdom in both ways and also that both ways require determination. You have to make the choice that works best for you. At the same time, you may find that those problems that crop up in an enduring marriage become less and less significant and are outweighed by the new and exciting things you discover through the years with your loved one.

Here are some nuggets of good advice that have helped others who were determined to make their marriages happy and long-lasting.

NEVER UNDERESTIMATE KINDNESS

204 When you don't know what to do, at least be kind. That was the solution for one Fabulous 400 dad. He said, "When my wife had a severe headache, I felt helpless. What could I do? She didn't even want me to commiserate. I decided that I just had to do something, so I took the kids to the park for an hour. When we returned, she said she felt so much better, not just because of the peace and quiet, but because she realized that I wanted to do something to help her." Kindly catering to the special needs of a mate can certainly be healing. Be determined to be kind.

STRIVE FOR MORE THAN MEDIOCRITY

205 Sometimes we're content just doing what everyone else is doing—keeping up with the Joneses. This can result in a marriage without any special spark. Occasionally be the innovator—break new ground, go out on a limb, try something the Joneses never even thought of. Your new idea could be a fresh approach to your morning greeting, a unique place to serve a meal, a surprising excursion, an outrageous gift, an innovative way of helping your community. As your legacy, don't leave things "as they were" but be determined to leave a mark of creativity and goodness.

No Downhill Slide Don't accept ⃝ **206** the idea that you reach a peak in your twenties and then just slide downhill. Dullness at any age can be stifling to your mate, family, and friends. If your marriage is going to last fifty years and more, you need to be growing wiser (and therefore more interesting) each year. Use a page in the back of your yearly calendar to note things you've achieved or learned during the year. Add to it regularly. If the page is blank, find the means of education that works best for you: self-education through reading and hobbies, taking adult education classes and field trips, or going out into the community and learning from volunteer work. Be determined to give your learning curve an uphill boost.

Whole Not Half Far too many ⃝ **207** spouses are so dependent on the skills of the other spouse that they can't cope alone. It's pitiful when one can't make dinner or the other can't add oil to the car! While you don't have to excel at all the things your spouse can do, you should be familiar with all of them. Keep honing your skills and have the determination to be a complete and remarkable person on your own. While two halves do make one whole, two wholes together are even better.

It's Not a Game There is a saying ⃝ **208** that marriage is a game played by two people. While there are some similarities such as the necessity to play by the rules, there should be no one winner in the game of marriage. Be determined that competitiveness (the stressful action of trying to outdo the other) has no place in marriage. Marriage is a proving ground for working and enjoying life *together*, not a "who shall be the greatest" tournament. Contentment and satisfaction should come from joint successes, not winner and loser situations.

209 **DON'T LEAVE HOME WITHOUT IT**   And that doesn't mean your credit card. Make the determination that parting will always be a ritual of love. More than telling where you're going and when you're returning, it should be filled with blessings and good wishes for each other, accompanied by holding hands, hugging, or kissing. This parting ritual doesn't take more than a minute (but it can!), and it's well worth it!

210 **THINKING AHEAD**   Too many spouses have good intentions but bad timing. (Oh, those dreaded words: "Sorry, I forgot it was your birthday.") Don't rely on special occasions to show your love. Daily: look for opportunities that will underscore how you care. Weekly: plan a special event together. Monthly: check your calendar for birthdays, anniversaries, and other dates for which you need to make advance preparations. Last-minute arrangements are better than none (and can occasionally be fun), but knowing that someone has thought ahead and planned ahead to make something special is a true sign of caring love. So be determined to think ahead!

211 **ONE AND ONLY**   Treat your spouse better—much better—than you treat anyone else. Certainly others among your family (and friends) will need all your attention at specific times. But in general, be determined that you will treat your beloved so well that there is no doubt that he or she is your one and only. It is supremely important to express your love; in fact, it may spur your partner to be more demonstrative.

212 **"I NEVER PROMISED YOU A ROSE GARDEN"**   This line can be of some comfort when times are tough. We can't predict the tragedies and the triumphs that lie ahead in a marriage. But we can develop the inner ability to come through the problems and continue living. One Fabulous 400 husband had really given his wife great cause for heartache over several years' time. In fact he used the excuse "I never promised you a rose garden" to alleviate his guilt. His wife stood by him through it all and when they finally worked out the problem and were once more a happy couple, he was determined to show his appreciation. One Saturday when she was away for the day, he actually planted a rose garden with a little path to the center where he placed an old-fashioned wrought-iron love seat. Covered with sweat and dirt, he finished this grand project just as she returned home to find that there was now a *real* rose garden in her honor! Today, a decade later, their house is still filled with bouquets of roses from that garden.

213 **LITTLE THINGS MEAN A LOT**   One couple are very determined to do small but significant good deeds for one another. She fills his car with gas, or makes a fire in the fireplace before serving a romantic dinner, or organizes all the nuts and bolts in his workshop, or quietly slips a brand new tie onto his tie rack. He buys tickets to operas she loves, or runs her a bubble bath and lights candles in the bathroom, or offers to manicure her nails, or sings her to sleep with soothing love songs. How long have they been doing such things? More than sixty years!

214 **IF NOT NOW, LATER**   Often the partners in a marriage desire something that's impossible to achieve at present. Rather than banish the idea into the chasm of the future, one couple showed a determination to accomplish their dream. They talked about it, read about it, and planned ahead for a Caribbean cruise that was financially out of the question for the foreseeable future. The wife took an unused round fishbowl and pasted the picture of a cruise boat on the front. Then she taped a sturdy lid on the bowl, and put a slit in it. She wrote on the lid "Contributions accepted for our future cruise." It took years, but spare coins and bills did add up to a fund that was used toward the much-wanted adventure.

215 **DON'T KEEP IT TO YOURSELF**   As the years pass, verbal expressions of approval for each other sometimes diminish. After all, our spouse is supposed to *know* how good (special, intelligent, good-looking, loved, witty) he or she is. In a marriage partnership, mum is *not* the word. Helping to build a feeling of self-worth in your mate is just as important as for your child. So don't be stingy with compliments. Remind your loved one often of the varied reasons you love him or her. Be determined to share your love at least once each day!

216 **NIX THE NEGATIVES**   As anniversaries pass and there are more shared experiences, there can be the tendency to be negative. Lines like "It will never work," "No one does that," "We tried that before," and "What a stupid suggestion," can squelch an otherwise good idea. Instead of being negative, make the determination to try lines such as "Let's try it," "It's possible," "How can we make it work?" and "That's different, but good." Unless an idea is immoral or illegal, consider it seriously. A can-do attitude is actually health-giving!

217 **A SCRAPBOOK OF LOVE**   Greeting cards are so expensive to buy! And they are often so beautiful and contain such lovely messages that it's a pity to just read them once and then throw them away. Here's a tradition you could start at anytime. One couple started a scrapbook of the cards they gave each other for birthdays, anniversaries, Valentine's Day, and other occasions. Some were bought, some handmade, all were loving. Making the scrapbook and keeping it current takes time and determination, but it is always up-to-date. On each anniversary, they sit down to share their scrapbook of love.

IF THERE IS JUST ONE NIGHT

218 The most magical night of the year should be your wedding anniversary. Make the determination that you won't ever let the day slip by without making it special. One couple return to the fast-food place where they had their first date. Another couple go dancing and request "their song" to be played. Another spend the night looking at videos of their wedding, the children, their houses, and trips. You can be forgiven many things in a marriage, but don't let failure to celebrate the wedding be one of them. When you get a new date book and calendar for the coming year, let your anniversary be your number one entry.

ALWAYS MORE TO LEARN

219 Don't let pride get in the way of improving your marriage. Maybe you think it's as good as it can get, but be determined to make it even better. One couple in my survey keep up-to-date by reading magazines and books on the subject and sharing some of these new ideas with one another. They readily admit that they went to counseling to get over a problem. Although their marriage is now very sound, they recommend going to a marriage retreat every few years. (These educational and romantic getaway weekends sponsored by churches and civic organizations specialize in practical solutions to the many challenges of marriage.) The wife describes it as a "tune up," and the husband says "it's like putting high octane gas in your car's tank!"

220 **DAY'S END JOURNAL**   Keep a small journal-style book on the night table. Write a sentence or two summing up your feelings about the day. Determine to be honest. Each one can write separately, or one can dictate and the other write it down. Even if the day has been a hectic one, the journal is a good way to communicate feelings and opinions to each other. It also brings a couple closer together because they see what was meaningful to the other as well as what wasn't such a great event. At the same time, they are enjoying a shared activity at the end of each day.

221 **THE LAST LOVE LETTER**   So often when a spouse dies, the other has feelings of guilt over things left unsaid. Be determined that this won't happen to you. One Fabulous 400 couple—now married over thirty years—has each written the other a love letter, saying and re-saying all the things they've felt through the years. The letters are sealed and put in the file with their wills. Whenever they wish, they are free to update this last love letter. While parting is sad, let there be no regrets for things said or unsaid. These letters are a fulfillment of a line in a poem by John Greenleaf Whittier: "For all of good the past hath had, Remains to make our own time glad . . . God's love and blessing, then and there, Are now and here and everywhere."

222 **MY BEST FRIEND**   The one you married should be your dearest and best friend, your one and only love. While you may not be a poet, here is a poem that lets you share all your feelings of love with your best friend. Consider writing it out in your own handwriting. Yes, it's copyrighted, but I'm giving you my permission and I'll never tell a soul that you didn't actually write it yourself!

LET ME BE YOUR FRIEND AND LOVER

Let me take your hand to walk together,
a loyal guide through life's stormy weather.

Let me win your heart and be your only love,
thanking God for you and blessings from above.

Let me hear with patience what you have to say,
the challenges we face each passing day.

Let me know the hurts and burdens that you've had,
giving my cheer to times when you've been sad.

Let me see your sparkling eyes and loving smile,
forgetting fears at least a little while.

Let me dance so close with you as one, not two,
remembering when our love was young and new.

Let me laugh with joy about the fun we've shared,
those little things that showed how much we cared.

Let me gently lead when you can't find the way,
to soothe and smooth the hard times of your day.

Let me share with you each day's joy and sorrow,
always looking for a bright tomorrow.

Let me be with you in sickness and in health,
your comfort in our poverty or wealth.

Let me be for you the one who's always near,
a vow for better or for worse, each year.

Let me be the one who thrills and fills your heart,
always together 'til death do us part.

Let me be forgiven foolish things I do,
wanting only happiness for you.

Let me be so close to you we breathe as one,
enfolded in your arms when day is done.

Let me love you alone, now and forever,
my best friend, my one and only lover.

Index